Love Good Food

Love Good Food

Sophie Michell

DUNCAN BAIRD PUBLISHERS

LONDON

LOVE GOOD FOOD
Sophie Michell

First published in the United Kingdom and Ireland in
2012 by
Duncan Baird Publishers Ltd
Sixth Floor, Castle House
75–76 Wells Street
London W1T 3QH

Conceived, created and designed by Duncan Baird
Publishers

Managing Editor: Grace Cheetham
Editors: Alison Bolus and Camilla Davis
Managing Designer: Manisha Patel
Designer: Gail Jones
Production: Uzma Taj
Commissioned photography: Toby Scott
Food Stylist: Jayne Cross
Prop Stylist: Tamsin Weston

British Library Cataloguing-in-Publication Data:
A CIP record for this book is available from the
British Library

ISBN: 978-1-84899-010-4

10 9 8 7 6 5 4 3 2 1

Typeset in Lisboa
Colour reproduction by XY Digital
Printed in China by Imago

Acknowledgments
Thank you to all the team at DBP, to my agents at Deborah
Mckenna and to my family for being so wonderful.

Publisher's note
While every care has been taken in compiling the recipes
for this book, Duncan Baird Publishers, or any other
persons who have been involved in working on this
publication, cannot accept responsibility for any errors
or omissions, inadvertent or not, that may be found in
the recipes or text, nor for any problems that may arise
as a result of preparing one of these recipes. If you are
pregnant or breastfeeding or have any special dietary
requirements or medical conditions, it is advisable to
consult a medical professional before following any of the
recipes contained in this book.

Notes on the Recipes
Unless otherwise stated:
Use medium eggs, fruit and vegetables
Use fresh ingredients, including herbs and chillies
Do not mix metric and imperial measurements
1 tsp = 5ml   1 tbsp = 15ml   1 cup = 250ml

To my grandmother, Ruth Hughes

Contents

Introduction

I have wanted to write this book for years. For me, food is all about love – love of the ingredients you can work with, the different cuisines and techniques that you can use, the tastes, textures and aromas you can serve up and the memories you can create.

These days we are bombarded with visions of food and chefs all the time: in magazines and books, and on websites and TV. Chefs create such amazing dishes in an instant, but we know that behind the scenes they have an army of minions and a huge, well-stocked professional kitchen supporting them. Yet despite knowing that, we long to achieve what they achieve, preferably with effortless ease. It is possible to make amazing dishes on your own at home – and I hope to show you that cooking is a fantastic and enjoyable way to spend your time. Cooking for family and friends is often one of the best ways of bringing people together. What could be more enjoyable than sharing good food, wine and conversation around the table?

MY BACKGROUND

I started working in kitchens aged 15, although for as long as my family can remember I had my head in cookbooks and my hands working with food. Since then I've worked in a great variety of professional kitchens, including some amazing high-end restaurants, some with Michelin-starred kitchens, where the cooking is like a form of alchemy. This is the most polished and perfect food you are ever likely to eat.

For the past 10 years, though, I have not always had the luxury of a professional kitchen behind me. During that time I have cooked for many events on location or have served up food on film sets, where the conditions can be primitive, to say the least. However, these less-than-perfect conditions do not mean that these clients haven't all wanted good restaurant-style food…. I just have to simplify my recipes to work in smaller environments and challenging conditions. At the other end of the scale, I have also cooked in private homes for the rich and famous in situations that bring their own, quite different, challenges.

This book is the result of my experience. It is full of beautiful and stunning recipes, written simply and plainly. There are no complicated terms and no OTT cheffy techniques, which can just as easily put people off as impress them. Inevitably, the recipes vary in the skill and time required to make them, and while some need only a handful of ingredients, others contain more, but they are all dishes that will be loved by everyone.

I am not pretending that this is a "ready in 30 minutes" type book, because many of the recipes are more complex than that. Also, I do want to stretch people's imagination a bit, as in the recipes for Tomato & Geranium Jellies with Crab & Micro Basil (see page 64), Summer Vegetable & Truffle Oil Pizzas (see page 130) and the Smoked Tea- & Star Anise-Braised Pork Ribs with Pickled Cucumber (see page 96), for example. I also want to take the mystique out of ingredients such as pea shoots, sumac and truffle oil, so that you are happy to use them when you cook at home.

COOKING AND EATING MY WAY AROUND THE WORLD

This book also reflects the other love of my life, apart from cooking, which is travelling, which has always been intertwined with my career in food. Throughout my travels around the world, I have discovered amazing dishes and ingredients.

Babi guling in Bali...

When I was 11, my family travelled around Bali and Australia for 8 months. I come from a very foody background, but this is where my eyes were really opened to a whole new world of food. I could not get over things like the lurid pink tapioca desserts sold on the roadside, the smells of chicken satay being grilled or the fact that the hotel pet monkey would pick us green coconuts to drink from.

We devoured our way through Bali: coconut banana pancakes with palm sugar for breakfast or *babi guling* (slow-roasted spiced suckling pig) in Ubud, next door to a dark temple with frangipani and incense heavy in the air.... Then later we'd have coconut oil-fried salty chips after swimming with spinner dolphins on the volcanic sandy beaches of Lovina or eat plates of dangerous barracuda (now spiced and grilled), which we had chased in the sea while snorkelling that morning. I have never forgotten those vibrant experiences.

Kangaroo steaks in Australia...

The magic continued in Australia. Where else could you find sushi, sashimi and miso soup next to fluffy American pancakes and bacon on a hotel breakfast buffet? Bondi Beach was where I had my first oyster. I hated it, and rarely ate them again till I was 19, when I suddenly fell in love with them and would consume them en masse while working in a fish restaurant in London.

We also tried kangaroo steaks and loved them, then went on to experience the best Mexican, Greek and Italian food in Melbourne (think steaming authentic fresh coriander- and lime-laced burritos, cinnamon-scented homemade moussakas and perfectly *al dente* spaghetti vongole....)

These travels subconsciously developed my love of combining flavours from different cultures, which is something that Australian chefs in particular do so well. In this book I want to show simple ways of cooking in this style. It can be a risky business mixing different food cultures together, but I love it when it is done properly. This is where dishes such as the Asian Beef Carpaccio with Micro Herbs (see page 46), which mixes Italian and South-East Asian flavours, or the Sesame Tuna with Pink Grapefruit Salad & Wasabi Potato Salad (see page 49) are highlights.

Polenta uncia and *sopressa* in Italy...

Years later, back in Europe I spent months on and off in Milan, Como and Monza in Italy, learning how to make proper Italian food at home, with an Italian mama. This is the best way to learn Italian cooking. Then I spent much of the rest of my time discovering the hidden restaurant gems in the area, learning even more. Each restaurant would specialize in one dish, so off we would go for platters of smoked cheese and pancetta risotto oozing off our forks or to a bio-farm restaurant with the best tagliata (rare steak). On another day, we would drive up to mountains for *polenta uncia* (polenta fried with garlic, cheese, butter and sage) and roasted rabbit, followed by shots of grappa. The fried polenta used here in the Venison Steaks with Pickled Red Cabbage & Truffle Polenta Fries (see page 112) is an adaptation of this.

In Aslo (just north of Venice), I discovered homemade *sopressa* (cured pork sausage) with mustard fruits (which star in the Ham Hock Terrine with Mustard Fruits on page 36) and local cheeses. On the way to Lake Garda, it was pumpkin and amaretti raviolis followed by grilled trout fresh from the water. Since then, beta-carotene-rich pumpkin and squash have become a staple part of our diet and show no sign of losing their continuing starring role. Try squash in the Butternut Squash, Chilli & Maple Syrup Soup (see page 28). I would often return to the UK with a suitcase full of fresh porcini mushrooms, which I found far more interesting to bring home than the fashionable shoes from Milan. Similarly, using Pecorino Sardo cheese in pesto is something I picked up when consulting for a cookery school in Sardinia.

Boureki and Sfakian cheese pies in Crete...

Ten years ago, my family moved to Crete. Greek food is hugely under-appreciated, but we ate really well there. It is a simple diet that relies on fresh seasonal produce. It hasn't really changed much over the centuries and is often hailed as the healthiest diet of the Med. This is where I first tried sea urchins, with their sweet iodine flavour, served chilled with lemon and olive oil. I made *boureki* (courgettes layered with mint, mizithra and tomato) at my friends' taverna, and discovered air-dried octopus, Sfakian cheese pies, chestnut stifado and braised wild greens with artichokes. Our renovated old house was the central village house and, in the old Kafenion tradition, still has an ancient wood-burning bread oven and grape pit. I was often transported back in time when sitting in the dappled sunlight and ancient-vine covered courtyard. You can feel that it has seen many a celebration dinner with friends and family.

Fattoush and *za'atar* breads in Beiruit...

Then recently, I spent a year in Beirut, consulting for a restaurant, which is where I learnt about the most romantic of flavours, such as rosewater, orange blossom, pomegranate, pistachio and sumac. These aromatic and jewel-like additions are part of my everyday cooking now in recipes such as Sea Bass Sashimi with Pomegranate and Micro Herbs (see page 52). I love the Lebanese mezze style of eating. *Fattoush*, pomegranate-caramelized chicken livers, baby birds, *hindbi* (wild chicory with fried onions) grilled halloumi, beetroot houmous, *shish taouk* (juicy chicken kebabs) and many beautiful lamb dishes were all served up and loved. Beetroot is a more versatile root veg than you might have thought. In addition to being used in houmous, I have used it to make a mousse (see page 75) and also borrowed its fantastic colour to make the most stunning gravlax: Beetroot-Cured Salmon Gravlax (see page 56). This is one of those dishes that is almost too beautiful to eat. Food becomes seriously fun when you start experimenting like this. As for ingredients such as *za'atar*, I started using it when I learned to make breads in the Beiruti mountains, not because the spice became fashionable in London.

LEARNING TO EXPERIMENT

People are often scared of the unknown, and inexperienced cooks will often revert back to the tried and tested methods and ingredients that they feel safe with. This is especially so when entertaining, because taking a chance on a new recipe containing unusual ingredients when you have guests coming might seem to be tempting fate. However, it is worth taking the plunge once in a while because when you master a new skill or really taste a new ingredient and learn where it can come into your daily life, it opens up a world of new ideas and creations. Similarly, be prepared to change or add an ingredient to a familiar dish and see what happens. This is how I created the Blood Orange Tart (see page 166), the Caramelized Coconut Rice Pudding (see page 154) and Pimm's Trifle (see page 156). For a savoury example, consider the Sour Cherry Meatballs with Buttery Tagliatelli on page 102. Always popular, meatballs are now appearing on menus everywhere, whether on their own with vegetables, in a sauce or in a pasta or rice dish, and it is so easy to make them exciting and unusual by adding some new ingredients, such as the sour cherries and pine nuts that I chose to use in my recipe.

Trying new or simply unfamiliar ingredients can be nerve wracking: investing money in an unknown product and not understanding how to use it can seem like a risk. I am sure we all have the odd pot of obscure spice or vinegar that we used for one recipe and never picked up again. However, it is only through experimenting that we develop our cooking skills and expand our repertoire, and in so doing learn to take the courage to be inventive. I am hoping that once you have tried some of the ingredients I have featured in this book, they will become part of your everyday cooking.

Here are some of the vegetables you might like to try: **Celeriac** can be used to make a wonderful mash (see page 205) if you fancy a change from potato. Not only is it low in carbohydrates, but it has a wonderful savoury flavour and is very versatile. **Fennel** is much underrated: it lends a subtle aniseed flavour to dishes such as Five-Spice Scallops with Fennel Purée & Orange Dressing (see page 61). **Chestnuts** are perfect for giving a dish a taste of winter. Try the Pork, Quince & Chestnut Casserole with Watercress Mash (see page 95) for the ultimate in comfort food on cold winter days. **Jerusalem artichokes** are quite unappealing to look at, but they make the most amazing soups and roasts. Their flavour is similar to that of globe artichokes, and they are great during the autumn and winter months. Try them in the Jerusalem Artichoke Soup with Sourdough Parmesan Croûtons (see page 29) and the Roasted Chicken Breast with Hazelnut & Jerusalem Artichoke Couscous (see page 83). **Swiss chard** is a leafy vegetable with either white or multicoloured stems. These greens make a change from the usual cabbage. Finally,

quince is an old-fashioned fruit tht is inedible in its raw state, but when cooked is wonderfully fragrant and deep pink. I love making jams and chutneys with it, but I also add it to savoury dishes, such as the Pork, Quince & Chestnut Casserole with Watercress Mash (see page 95).

Many of the new storecupboard ingredients you will find in my recipes are there as a result of my travels. Since living in Beirut I have a few ingredients that will always be in my cupboard:

Pomegranate molasses is what I now use in preference to aged balsamic vinegar. It adds a little sweetness and sourness to dishes. It is great with lemon juice and olive oil in salad dressings, it glazes meat and it also adds balance to casseroles and rice dishes. I have used it to give a wonderful flavour to the Halloumi, Quinoa, Pomegranate & Mint Salad (see page 67).

Za'atar is a wonderful Middle Eastern mixture of herbs and spices. It changes its recipe according to the region, but mine is the classic Lebanese mix of toasted sesame seeds, dried thyme, fresh thyme, sumac, sea salt and pepper. I use za'atar for flavouring breads in the Za'atar Flatbreads (see page 179), mixing with oils or yogurt for dips and sprinkling on chicken and lamb before cooking. You can make your own mix.

Sumac is actually a small astringent pink berry, not a spice. It is ground up and sprinkled over salads and various other dishes, adding an almost citrus flavour. I have used it in the Lamb Skewers with Lentil Salad on page 100. Sumac can be found at large supermarkets, or in Middle Eastern delis.

Cassia bark is my other spice to introduce. Cassia is very similar to cinnamon in flavour and in appearance, though it's a touch more spicy and has a hint of musk to it. I love the huge curled bark; it's really beautiful. You can use cinnamon instead if you cannot get hold of it. If you want to experiment with cassia, try the Cassia-Scented Custard Tart with Apple Compote (see page 155).

Rosewater and orange blossom water are the two most romantic and whimsical ingredients in my opinion. Although I have been using them for years, they still transport me straight back to the Middle East, where I can picture myself in the searing heat of a summer's day, cooled only by fresh homemade lemonade mixed with mint leaves, rosewater and crushed ice, or eating orange blossom pastries served after dark during Ramadan. I add rosewater to desserts and Persian rice dishes, whilst orange blossom adds a wonderful touch to sweets. They can both be found in most supermarkets. I used orange blossom water to ring the changes on that old favourite, the chocolate éclair, which we have known and loved for generations, to make the Orange Blossom Éclairs (see page 184). The result is a delicate and exotic treat.

My time in Italy also introduced me to many new ingredients, some of which have since become firm favourites and will be found in my recipes.

Truffle oil may seem very luxurious, but I highly recommend buying a little bottle of it. Drops and drizzles of it can transform food. You'll be amazed how much it raises the game when added to cauliflower soup, simple mash or risottos.... I have used it to great effect in the Venison Steaks with Pickled Red Cabbage & Truffle Polenta Fries (see page 112) and the Summer Vegetable & Truffle Oil Pizzas (see page 130).

As for ***mostarda di frutta***, or mustard fruits, this is basically a condiment to have with cold meats, cheese and salamis. These jewel-like preserves consist of whole candied fruits suspended in a sugar syrup and flavoured with mustard oil. They are both beautiful and tasty. You can buy them online, in Italian delis and in some supermarkets.

LOOKING BACK TO OUR PAST

Many ingredients that were used in times past are now enjoying a new-found popularity. **Spelt** is a great grain to introduce into your diet. It's an ancient form of wheat that is more easily digestable for people with a wheat intolerance, so it is good from that aspect, plus I love the nutty flavour and texture. It's quite fashionable now and is just lovely when made into a risotto, such as the Spelt & Roast Butternut Squash Risotto (see page 133): its rounded nuttiness is comfort food at its best.

Quinoa, amaranth and millet, other ancient and exotic grains, are making a welcome comeback. Quinoa, much loved by the Aztecs, is a great grain to include in your diet. It is high in protein and contains amino acids and more nutrients than, say, couscous or rice. Plus its flavour and appearance are unique. So try it in the Halloumi, Quinoa, Pomegranate & Mint Salad (see page 67). Try experimenting with many grains to see how they will fit into your cooking and what their different qualities are. Trying out new ingredients like this, mixing and matching them with old favourites to create interesting new dishes is the joy of cooking.

Samphire is quite under-used, but it really tastes amazing. It is named after the patron saint of fishermen, Saint Peter, or "Saint Pierre", which evolved into "Sainpierre" and then to "Samphire". It has a great, salty, fresh flavour and is also known as "sea asparagus". It is perfect steamed with seafood and served lightly buttered. You can buy it in some supermarkets and fishmongers. I have used it in the Potted Shrimp & Samphire Tarts (see page 54).

NOT ALL GOOD FOOD HAS TO BE EXPENSIVE

However, this book isn't just about expensive or exotic ingredients. I have made some dishes using cheaper cuts of meat to prove that fantastic food can be made with all sorts of ingredients. One of the more unknown cuts is hanger steak. Hanger steak is a very cheap and tasty cut. It is under-appreciated in Britain, where it is called "skirt". I often have it in Paris under the name of *onglet*, where it is usually served as *Steak frites* and comes with fries and garlic butter. It must not be over cooked, as it will go tough, and it also works well with marinades. Pork belly is another flavoursome, budget-conscious favourite that I have glazed with miso in another one of the dishes: Miso-Glazed Pork Belly with Stir-Fried Bok Choy on page 92.

TAKING A MODERN LOOK AT FOOD

The other aspect to this book is to take a modern look at food, which is where micro herbs come in. For years it's been the fashion to pile up a mix of micro herbs on a plate in restaurants. In fact, micro herbs and the flavours they contribute should be handled with more respect than normal herbs. They are stronger in taste and can add a powerful punch along with undeniable beauty. Knowing which one is good with the right ingredients is important. Micro herbs make a fantastic difference to recipes; try the Herb Consommé (see page 26), Asian Beef Carpaccio with Micro Herbs (see page 46) and Pan-Fried Sea Bass with Micro Herb & Pepper Salad (see page 115).

As for pea shoots, with their bright green chlorophyll leaves and delicate fronds, these are great to use in soups, salads and various other dishes. You can also find them in most supermarkets now. They really are so beautiful to work with and add a fresh spring look to any dish. Also, just see how versatile they are from the following recipes I have used them in: Pea Shoot & Watercress Soup (see page 22), Pea Shoot Pancakes with Crispy Pancetta & Sweet Chilli Sauce (see page 35) and Potato Gnocchi with Pea-Shoot Pesto & Pecorino Shavings (see page 137). All of these dishes have been lifted out of the ordinary by the presence of the pea shoots.

I love dishes that look fresh and clean, such as the Chargrilled Prawns with Mango (see page 129) and the Tomato & Geranium Jellies with Crab & Micro Basil (see page 64). Simple, but immensely appealing. Also eye-catching, but this time because of their bright colours, are dishes such as Chargrilled Chicken, Beetroot, Manchego & Candied Pecan Salad (see page 30) and Spiced Lamb Flatbreads (see page 43). For sheer beauty, Beetroot-Cured Salmon Gravlax (see page 56) is unbeatable. This dish uses edible flowers, which have been my passion since I was a child: crystallized rose petals, violets, micro-borage flowers, pansies... they all seem to add magic.

My final favourite for extra drama is edible gold, in the form of gold leaf and gold dust. These little pots of gilt are quite easy to buy online, and can also be found in cake shops and some supermarkets, and have garnished dishes in the Middle East and India for some time. A little goes a long way and they really leave an impact. Everything tastes better covered in gold....

NEW TECHNIQUES TO TRY

I want you to learn some new and varied cooking styles in this book, so throughout I have endeavoured to show you how to follow techniques that might at first seem complicated, such as making a twice-baked soufflé (see page 76), but are in fact very do-able. Once you've mastered the techniques, all the dishes will be within your grasp. In the light meals chapter, I show you how to clarify a stock and make a consommé (see page 26), and these techniques can be applied to lots of different flavours and clear soups. I also show you how to make a terrine (see page 36); terrines are a joy to make and very simple. I love the unveiling and slicing of a new terrine, and they come into their own for celebration dinners. In addition, I show you how to make ceviche (see page 53), where the fish is cured by the citrus juices, and cure salmon (see page 56). In the the main meals chapter I show you how to cook the perfect risotto (see page 133), make your own ravioli (see page 134) and gnocchi (see page 137) and prepare light-as-a-feather tempura (see page 139). Moving on to sweet dishes, in the desserts chapter I show you how to make the perfect English custard (see page 156). Finally we move to the baking chapter, where you will learn how to make choux pastry for Orange Blossom Éclairs (see page 184), enriched doughs (sticky buns), flatbreads and light-as-air sponges, such as the Iced Fancies (see page 186)

Learning new skills from different countries is what excites me more than anything else. Searing and finely slicing meats, as in the Asian Beef Carpaccio with Micro Herbs (see page 46), can be applied to many different meats and fish, and the method of making a semifreddo, for example, can be changed according to the season. I have added a twist to the Lemon Meringue Cupcakes (see page 191) by replacing the buttercream topping with meringue, whilst in the Mayan Chocolate Cupcakes (see page 192) I've added a wake-up call to the tastebuds with chilli and pink peppercorns, to make a cupcake with a surprising sting in its tail.

Another currently popular type of food that has caught my attention is moreish wraps and sandwiches, plus all sorts of ethnic street food. These dishes are really the ones that create cravings, and I love serving a selection when I have friends over. I have devised some fantastic examples of food to be eaten on the go: check out the Chicken Tikka Chapatis (see page 32), Lobster Rolls with Pea Shoots (see page 66), Vietnamese Beef Spring Rolls (see page 45), Cauliflower & Onion Pakoras with Mango & Fenugreek Salsa (see page 70) and Chorizo, Sweet Potato & Coriander Quesadillas (see page 44) as just some examples. Use these recipes as starting points for your own innovative food-on-the-go.

HEALTHY FOOD

This is my fourth cookbook and it is the first book I have written where the emphasis is not on healthy eating and diet food. This doesn't mean that I don't always try to keep an overriding sense of freshness and cleanness to my food, and although these aren't diet recipes they are still pretty health conscious. Eating well is not about starving yourself. My biggest piece of advice to anyone is make as much of your food from scratch as possible, because cooking your own food is the fastest route to a better diet.

This even applies to desserts: making a humdinger of a cake or pudding from scratch will not only enable you to realize how much fat and sugar goes into these dishes, but it will also make for a more satisfying meal. Shop-bought "goodies" are simply full of hidden nasties. I find the Rich Flourless Chocolate Cake (see page 190) unbelievably satisfying, even with just a small slice.

All the recipes in this book focus on using good ingredients and fresh new ways to prepare them as purely as possible, with Chargrilled Prawns with Mango (see page 129) being a good example.

At a very simplistic level, colour can be a good indicator of how healthy a plate of food is. Have you ever noticed how beige and bland-looking junk food can often be? If you bring in lots of veggies, herbs and spices, they add a burst of flavour on the palate and a colour to the plate. Look at the Superfood Salad with Avocado & Lemon Dressings on page 68 – it's a rainbow salad and full of so many top, nutrient-rich ingredients – or Saffron-Poached Chicken with Parsley & Tarragon Gremolata (see page 84). They really boost your spirits as well as your health.

I have always looked at food as more than just fuel. I am a great believer that the ingredients we consume make a huge difference to our mind and bodies. This is why these recipes include ingredients like salmon, sardines and tuna for their omega-3 oils and chicken, turkey and venison for their low-fat protein. That is not to say that we shouldn't indulge sometimes, as life is too short not to love good food. This cookbook is not focused on diet, but it is focused on good ingredients and great cooking methods.

I find now that the methods of cooking I often use tend to be lighter and healthier. I very rarely make creamy, heavy sauces or gravies, preferring herb-spiked dressings, as in the Marinated Hanger Steak with Sweet Potato Mash and Coriander-Honey Dressing (see page 106) or the Roast Chicken with Salsa Verde (see page 88), and will often replace the traditional carbohydrates with vegetables. Also, taking inspiration from Asia means I use all those vibrant, immune system-boosting ingredients like ginger, chilli and garlic; plus the Asian cooking styles, which are often low in fat, come into their own.

DIVE IN AND ENJOY!

I have divided the book into chapters containing light meals, main meals, desserts and baking. The light meals section really indicates light meals, starters or dishes you can mix and match and serve up a few at a time. The main meals are more substantial, but to be honest they are all quite interchangeable and I like the idea of mezze: eating lots of different flavours in one meal.

With new ingredients to discover across the world, and many old or even ancient ones that have been rediscovered to try, plus new combinations, new cooking methods and just new ways of looking at food, now is an exciting time to be cooking. Forget the rigid rules and elitism of yesteryear, and be prepared to embrace a modern take, with new flavour combinations and different ingredients.

I have loved writing these recipes and all the experimenting that went into them. I hope you will enjoy making them and eating them, and I also hope that some will become firm favourites. Ultimately, I want you, too, to "Love Good Food"....

Sophie Michell x

Light Meals

Pea Shoot & Watercress Soup

PREPARATION TIME: 15 minutes | COOKING TIME: 25 minutes | SERVES: 4

1 tbsp olive oil
1 onion, finely chopped
2 leeks, trimmed and
    finely sliced
1.25l/44fl oz/5 cups
    vegetable stock
200g/7oz pea shoots,
    roughly chopped
75g/2½oz watercress,
    roughly chopped
freshly grated nutmeg,
    to taste
sea salt and freshly
    ground black pepper

This is my healthy detox soup for the times when I want something comforting but packed full of goodness. The watercress gives it a lovely peppery flavour and the pea shoots add even more iron as well as antioxidants.

Heat the oil in a large saucepan over a medium-low heat. Add the onion and leeks, then cook gently, covered, for 8 minutes until softened and translucent. Stir frequently and be careful not to let the onion and leek burn, as this will ruin the flavour. Pour in the stock and bring to the boil, then reduce the heat to low and simmer for 10 minutes.

Add the pea shoots and watercress and cook for a further 5 minutes. Remove from the heat and, using a hand-held stick blender, or transferring the mixture to a blender or food processor, blitz until smooth. Reheat the soup until hot and season with nutmeg, salt and pepper.

Spring Minestrone

PREPARATION TIME: 20 minutes | COOKING TIME: 30 minutes | SERVES: 4

1 tbsp olive oil
100g/3½oz pancetta,
  diced
1 onion, finely chopped
2 garlic cloves, finely
  chopped
3 celery sticks, finely
  diced
1 leek, finely diced
1 courgette, diced
50g/1¾oz French beans,
  cut into 2.5cm/1in
  pieces
1l/35fl oz/4 cups
  vegetable stock
a large pinch of oregano
100g/3½oz broccoli
  florets
100g/3½oz asparagus
  tips
sea salt and freshly
  ground black pepper

TO SERVE
1 small handful of
  micro basil leaves
1 small handful of
  Parmesan cheese
  shavings

Minestrone is a classic and very versatile vegetable soup. I add more root veggies and pulses during winter and more tomatoes during summer, making it the ultimate seasonal soup. This recipe is a rarefied version, using some lovely delicate spring vegetables.

Heat the oil in a large saucepan over a medium-high heat. Add the pancetta and cook, stirring frequently, for 5 minutes, then reduce the heat to medium-low and add the onion, garlic, celery and leek. Cook for 10 minutes until the onion is softened and translucent.

Add the courgette and French beans and cook for a further 5 minutes, then add the stock and oregano and bring to the boil. Reduce the heat to low and simmer gently for 5 minutes. Add the broccoli and asparagus and simmer for a further 5 minutes.

Remove from the heat and season with salt and pepper. Serve immediately sprinkled with a little micro basil and scattered with Parmesan shavings.

Herb Consommé

PREPARATION TIME: 25 minutes | COOKING TIME: 20 minutes | SERVES: 4

1 boneless, skinless
   chicken breast
1 small handful of parsley
1 small handful of
   tarragon
1 garlic clove
1 leek, roughly chopped
2 carrots, peeled and
   roughly chopped
1 celery stick, roughly
   chopped
1 small onion, roughly
   diced
1l/35fl oz/4 cups chicken
   stock
4 egg whites, lightly
   whisked
sea salt and freshly
   ground black pepper

TO SERVE
1 tbsp finely chopped
   chives
1 small handful of
   micro tarragon
1 small handful of
   micro basil
1 small handful of
   micro mint

To be able to clarify a stock is a classic skill and quite old school. I have included it in this book because a clear, golden, flavoursome stock is an item of beauty, and with the addition of micro herbs it forms a delicate prelude to any meal.

Put the chicken breast, parsley, tarragon, garlic and all the vegetables in a blender or food processor and blitz until finely chopped.

Pour the stock into a large saucepan and heat over a medium-high heat. When the stock is hot, stir in the egg whites and the chicken and vegetable mix. Bring to the boil, stirring continuously to stop the egg whites sinking to the bottom of the pan or sticking to the sides.

As soon as the stock begins to boil, stop stirring and reduce the heat to medium-low. Simmer, uncovered, for 15 minutes, then remove from the heat. A layer of chicken and egg white will form a "lid" on the surface of the liquid. When it does, make a small hole in the centre to let out the steam.

Using a ladle, carefully scoop out the clear liquid and pass it through a fine sieve, ideally lined with muslin cloth, into a clean pan. Season with salt and pepper and very gently reheat until almost boiling.

Mix the chives and micro herbs together and sprinkle some over each bowl of soup before serving.

Butternut Squash, Chilli & Maple Syrup Soup

PREPARATION TIME: **15 minutes** | COOKING TIME: **45 minutes** | SERVES: **4**

1 tbsp olive oil
1 onion, roughly chopped
2 garlic cloves, finely
    chopped
1 tsp dried chilli flakes
1 rosemary sprig
500g/1lb 2oz peeled and
    deseeded butternut
    squash, cut into cubes
1 litre/35fl oz/4 cups
    vegetable stock
1 tsp maple syrup
sea salt and freshly
    ground black pepper

TO SERVE
crème fraîche

This soup is a smooth, unassuming and quietly comforting bowl. I like to add a little chilli and rosemary for a savoury note and the maple syrup for sweet caramel undertones. It's very easy to make.

Heat the oil in a large saucepan over a medium-low heat. Add the onion and garlic and cook gently, covered, so the juices sweat out, for 8 minutes until softened and translucent. Stir frequently and be careful that the onion and garlic don't burn. Add the chilli flakes, rosemary and butternut squash, replace the lid and continue to cook for a further 5 minutes.

Pour in the stock and bring to the boil. Reduce the heat to low and simmer, covered, for 30 minutes until the squash is soft.

Remove the saucepan from the heat and take out the rosemary sprig. Add the maple syrup and season with salt and pepper. Using a hand-held stick blender, or transferring the mixture to a blender or food processor, blitz until very smooth. Reheat the soup until hot, then serve with a generous spoonful of crème fraîche swirled into each bowl.

Jerusalem Artichoke Soup with Sourdough Parmesan Croûtons

PREPARATION TIME: 25 minutes | COOKING TIME: 40 minutes | SERVES: 4

300g/10½oz Jerusalem
  artichokes
squeeze of lemon juice
1½ tsp olive oil
1 onion, finely chopped
1l/35fl oz/4 cups
  vegetable stock
100ml/3½fl oz/scant
  ½ cup double cream
sea salt and freshly
  ground black pepper

CROÛTONS
3 slices of sourdough
  bread
1 tbsp olive oil
25g/1oz Parmesan
  cheese, grated

Jerusalem artichokes have a nutty flavour, very similar to globe artichokes. They look knobbly and uninviting when raw, but produce a wonderfully smooth soup. The sourdough croûtons are chewy, crispy and cheesy all in one bite.

To prepare the Jerusalem artichokes, first fill a large bowl with cold water and add a good squeeze of lemon juice. Peel the artichokes with a small knife or swivel-bladed potato peeler, then slice them thinly and immediately put the slices in the prepared water. This will prevent the artichokes from oxidizing and turning black, which happens very quickly.

Heat the oil in a large saucepan over a medium-low heat. Add the onion and cook gently, covered, so the juices sweat out, for 8 minutes until softened and translucent. Stir frequently and be careful the onion doesn't burn. Pour in the stock, drain the artichokes and add to the pan, then bring to the boil. Reduce the heat to low and simmer, covered, for 30 minutes.

Meanwhile, to make the croûtons, heat the grill until very hot. Cut the crusts off the sourdough and discard, then cut the bread into cubes. Put the bread cubes on a baking tray, drizzle with the oil and sprinkle over the Parmesan. Put the tray under the grill and toast, tossing occasionally, for 10 minutes until golden and crispy. Leave to one side to cool.

Remove the soup from the heat and, using a hand-held stick blender, food processor or blender, blitz until very smooth. Add the cream and season with salt and pepper. Reheat the soup until hot and serve immediately, topped with the croûtons.

Chargrilled Chicken, Beetroot, Manchego & Candied Pecan Salad

PREPARATION TIME: 15 minutes | COOKING TIME: 30 minutes | SERVES: 4

8 small raw beetroot, scrubbed
1 tbsp olive oil
4 boneless, skinless chicken breasts
25g/1oz butter
100g/3½oz/1 cup pecan nuts
50g/1¾oz/heaped ¼ cup soft light brown sugar
1 large head of endive, trimmed and broken into leaves
2 heads of raddichio, trimmed and broken into leaves
100g/3½oz Manchego cheese shavings
sea salt and freshly ground black pepper

DRESSING
1 tsp Dijon mustard
1 tbsp white wine vinegar
3 tbsp olive oil
2 tsp walnut oil

I love serving this modern bistro-style salad for a light lunch. The deep pink beetroot, bitter endive and sweet crunchy nuts form a perfectly balanced dish and the colours are beautiful.

Preheat the oven to 200°C/400°F/Gas 6. Put the beetroot in a baking tin, drizzle with the oil and season with salt and pepper. Cover the tin with foil, then put in the oven and roast for 30 minutes, or until cooked through. Remove from the oven and leave until cool enough to handle. Using kitchen gloves to avoid turning your hands and nails pink, slide off the skins and cut the beetroot into quarters.

Meanwhile, heat a ridged griddle pan over a medium-high heat and cook the chicken breasts for about 6 minutes on each side until golden brown and cooked through. To test if they are ready, insert the tip of a sharp knife into the thickest part of the breast – the juices should run clear. Put the breasts on a plate, cover with foil and leave to one side to rest.

Melt the butter in a frying pan over a medium heat until it begins to foam. Add the pecans and cook for 3 minutes, turning occasionally, then add the sugars and cook for a further 3 minutes until golden and caramelized. Remove from the heat and leave to one side to cool slightly.

To make the dressing, whisk all the ingredients together in a small bowl until thoroughly combined. Put the endive, raddichio and beetroot into a large bowl and toss together, then toss through the dressing.

Cut each of the chicken breasts on the diagonal into 3–5 slices and arrange on piles of the salad leaves. Scatter over the Manchego shavings and the candied pecans and serve.

Chicken Tikka Chapatis

PREPARATION TIME: 15 minutes, plus 2 hours marinating time | COOKING TIME: 10 minutes | SERVES: 4

2 boneless, skinless
   chicken breasts, cut
   into strips
1 heaped tbsp tikka paste
1 tbsp natural yogurt
4 wholemeal chapatis
2–3 tbsp mango chutney
sea salt and freshly
   ground pepper

HERB & CHICKPEA
YOGURT
2 heaped tbsp roughly
   chopped mint leaves
2 heaped tbsp roughly
   chopped coriander
   leaves
½ tsp cumin seeds
150g/5½oz/scant ⅔ cup
   natural yogurt
100g/3½oz/½ cup
   drained, tinned
   chickpeas

These grab-and-go wonders are fab for packed lunches and quick bites. I kid you not: everyone loves these wraps and they get gobbled up within minutes.

Put the chicken in a large bowl and toss with the tikka paste and yogurt until the chicken is well coated. Cover with clear film and put in the fridge to marinate for 2 hours (or longer if this is more convenient).

Meanwhile, make the yogurt dip. Mix together the mint, coriander, cumin seeds and yogurt in a large bowl until thoroughly combined. Cover with clear film and put in the fridge until required.

When you are ready to eat, heat the grill until very hot. Put the chicken strips on a baking tray, season with salt and pepper and grill for about 10 minutes, turning occasionally, until cooked through. Meanwhile, add the chickpeas to the yogurt dip and mix until thoroughly combined.

Spread a thick layer of mango chutney on top of the chapatis, then top with the herb and chickpea yogurt. Divide the grilled chicken among the chapatis, then roll up and serve.

Warm Duck & Lychee Salad

PREPARATION TIME: 20 minutes | COOKING TIME: 2 hours | SERVES: 4

4 duck legs
5cm/2in piece of root
   ginger, peeled and
   finely chopped
200g/7oz drained,
   tinned lychees
4 spring onions, finely
   sliced
½ head of Chinese
   cabbage, thickly sliced
sea salt and freshly
   ground black pepper

DRESSING
1 tsp sesame seeds
1 red chilli, finely diced
2 tsp soy sauce
½ tsp sesame oil
1 tsp Chinese rice wine
   vinegar

Slow-roasted duck legs are great for making a fairly cheap but very tasty salad; I love the contrast between the sweet lychees and the savoury duck. With the addition of herbs and chilli, it really is a great salad to have as a lunch or as part of a big Asian feast.

Preheat the oven to 160°C/315°F/Gas 2–3. Season the duck legs generously with salt, then put them in a deep baking tray and scatter over the ginger. Cover with foil and put in the oven to roast for 1½ hours, then turn the oven temperature up to 200°C/400°F/Gas 6, remove the foil and cook for a further 30 minutes, or until the duck is browned and the meat easily pulls away from the bone. Remove the duck from the oven and leave to cool slightly.

Using two forks, shred the duck meat into small pieces and put in a bowl. Mix through a little of the fat, for flavour, plus the ginger, and season with salt and pepper. Leave to cool a little more, then add the lychees, spring onions and Chinese cabbage and toss until well combined.

Whisk together all the dressing ingredients in a small bowl, then pour over the duck and lychee salad and toss until all the ingredients are well coated. Serve immediately.

Pea Shoot Pancakes with Crispy Pancetta & Sweet Chilli Sauce

PREPARATION TIME: 20 minutes | COOKING TIME: 20 minutes | MAKES: 8 pancakes

50g/1¾oz pea shoots, plus extra to scatter
5 tbsp double cream
1 egg
75g/2½oz/¾ cup self-raising flour
½ tsp sugar
150g/5½oz/1 cup frozen peas, defrosted and roughly crushed
8 slices of pancetta or rashers of streaky bacon, cut into fine strips
50g/1¾oz butter
generous 3 tbsp sweet chilli sauce or chilli jam
sea salt and freshly ground black pepper

TO SERVE
100g/3½oz/generous ⅓ cup crème fraîche

These bright green pancakes, which are a novel take on brunch pancakes, are a real showstopper. I also make them bite sized for canapés, and sometimes top them with smoked salmon and chives instead of the pancetta and chilli sauce.

Put the pea shoots in a blender or food processor and blitz until finely chopped. Add the cream, egg, flour and sugar, then blitz again to form a smooth batter. Season with salt and pepper and fold in the peas.

Heat the grill until hot and put the pancetta on a baking tray. Grill the pancetta for 4 minutes until crispy, then turn over and cook on the other side for the same time. Leave to one side, covered with foil to keep warm.

Heat a large frying pan over a medium heat, then melt 1 tablespoon of the butter in the pan. Add 4 tablespoons of pancake batter to the pan, leaving enough space between each addition to allow for spreading. Cook the pancakes for 3 minutes on each side until golden brown. Remove the pancakes to a plate lined with kitchen paper and cover with a tea towel to keep warm. Repeat with the remaining batter, adding more butter to the pan as required.

Serve the pancakes with the pancetta on top and chilli sauce drizzled over. Add a dollop of crème fraîche, and scatter over the remaining pea shoots.

Ham Hock Terrine with Mustard Fruits

PREPARATION TIME: 25 minutes, plus overnight setting time | COOKING TIME: 2½ hours | SERVES: 10

2 ham hocks, about
2.5kg/5lb 8oz in total
1 onion, quartered
2 carrots, peeled and
roughly chopped
2 celery sticks, roughly
chopped
1 bouquet garni
4 peppercorns
2 tsp white wine vinegar
2 shallots, roughly
chopped
1 large bunch of parsley,
finely chopped
2 gelatine sheets
100g/3½oz mustard
fruits in their syrup
sea salt and freshly
ground black pepper

TO SERVE
150g/5½oz rocket leaves
toasted sourdough or
rustic white bread

Ham hocks are cheap and full of flavour. They take a little cooking but make great terrines, salads and soups. I have accompanied this terrine with *mostarda di frutta* (mustard fruits).

Put the ham hocks, onion, carrots, celery, bouquet garni and peppercorns in a large saucepan and cover with water. Bring to the boil, then reduce the heat to low and simmer for 2 hours or until the meat is falling off the bone. Leave to one side until the meat is cool enough to handle, then remove it from the bones and shred into smaller pieces. Cover with clear film and leave to one side.

Remove the vegetables and any remaining bones from the stock pot, then simmer over a low heat for 30 minutes, or until the stock has reduced to about 400ml/14fl oz/generous 1½ cups. Don't allow the stock to bubble too much, or it will turn cloudy. Stir in the vinegar, shallots and parsley and season with salt and pepper.

Cover the sides and base of a 900g/2lb loaf tin with 2 layers of clear film, leaving plenty of extra clear film over the sides to cover the top of the mixture once filled. Put the gelatine sheets in a small bowl of cold water and soak for about 5 minutes until softened, then squeeze to remove any excess water and stir into the stock until dissolved.

Press the shredded meat into the prepared loaf tin and pour over the stock. Cover with the clear-film flaps and put in the fridge for 30 minutes to set. Cut a piece of cardboard to fit snugly on top of the terrine, then weight the cardboard down on top of the terrine with cans of food or something else that is heavy, and return it to the fridge to set overnight. Slice the terrine and put on the plates with the mustard fruits. Serve with rocket leaves and toasted bread.

"These jewel-like mustard fruits add colour and piquancy to any dish."

Broad Bean, Pea Shoot & Parma Ham Salad with Truffle Dressing

PREPARATION TIME: 15 minutes, plus 15 minutes defrosting time | SERVES: 4

150g/5½oz/1 cup frozen broad beans, defrosted
150g/5½oz/1 cup frozen peas, defrosted
2 heads of Little Gem lettuce, trimmed and broken into leaves
12 slices of Parma ham
sea salt and freshly ground black pepper

TRUFFLE DRESSING
1 tsp Dijon mustard
4 tsp white wine vinegar
generous 3 tbsp olive oil
a splash of truffle oil
1 tsp chopped truffle paste (optional)

TO SERVE
30g/1oz pea shoots
20g/¾oz Parmesan cheese shavings

This salad is brought into the realms of gourmet food with the addition of the truffle oil dressing. Broad beans are great when popped out of their little casings, and the Parma ham with Parmesan shavings finish off the dish.

To make the dressing, whisk all the ingredients together in a small bowl until thoroughly combined. Leave to one side to let the flavours develop.

Pop the defrosted broad beans out of their pale outer skins and mix with the peas in a large bowl. Add the lettuces, then drizzle over the dressing and mix well. Season with salt and pepper.

Divide the lettuce leaves and the pea and bean mixture onto four serving plates. Arrange the Parma ham on top, scatter with pea shoots and Parmesan shavings, and serve.

Feta, Sun-Blush Tomato & Pancetta Mini Frittatas

PREPARATION TIME: 15 minutes | COOKING TIME: 15 minutes | MAKES: 4

olive oil, for greasing
8 slices of pancetta
200g/7oz feta cheese,
    crumbled
25g/1oz basil leaves, torn
12 sun-blush tomatoes,
    drained
10 eggs
100ml/3½fl oz/scant
    ½ cup milk
sea salt and freshly
    ground black pepper

Frittatas are great: they are quick and easy to make and you can be quite creative with them. Try different cheeses, herbs and meats to ring the changes. Children love these protein-packed bites for snacks and in lunch boxes.

Preheat the oven to 200°C/400°F/Gas 6. Grease four ramekins and line them with the pancetta. Stand them in a shallow tin.

Put an equal quantity of the feta into each of the ramekins. Divide the basil leaves into the ramekins and put 3 sun-blush tomatoes, cut-side facing up, in each one.

Whisk the eggs and milk together in a large bowl and season with salt and pepper. Pour the mixture into a jug for ease of use, then pour it into the ramekins.

Put the tin in the oven and bake for 15 minutes, or until the frittatas are just set and starting to brown. Remove from the oven and leave to cool in the ramekins, then remove and serve warm or cold.

Note that if you would rather make 6 smaller frittatas, use a 6-cup muffin tin and divide the ingredients equally into the cups.

Spiced Lamb Flatbreads

PREPARATION TIME: 40 minutes, plus making the dough | COOKING TIME: 30 minutes | SERVES: 4

1 tbsp olive oil
1 onion, finely chopped
2 garlic cloves, finely
    chopped
400g/14oz lamb mince
½ tsp ground cinnamon
½ ground allspice
a pinch of ground cumin
a pinch of ground
    coriander
1 tbsp tomato purée
1 tbsp pomegranate
    molasses, plus extra
    to drizzle (optional)
1 recipe quantity
    Flatbreads dough
    (see page 202)
flour, for dusting
3 tbsp pine nut kernels
1 small handful of micro
    mint leaves
100g/3½oz pomegranate
    seeds or the seeds
    tapped out of
    1 pomegranate
sea salt and freshly
    ground black pepper

When I lived in Beirut, I used to buy these flatbreads straight out of the oven from a hole-in-the-wall takeaway place near my house. The food was fabulous there and I still miss it...

Heat the oil in a large saucepan over a medium heat. Add the onion, garlic and lamb and stir until well combined. Cover the pan with a tight-fitting lid and cook for 10 minutes, stirring occasionally, until the ingredients start to turn golden and come together. Add the spices and tomato purée and season with salt and pepper. Stir in the pomegranate molasses, then remove the pan from the heat.

Preheat the oven to 180°C/350°F/Gas 4. Take the flatbreads dough from the fridge and turn out onto a lightly floured surface. Roll the dough into a ball, then divide into 8 pieces (for medium-sized flatbreads) or 24 pieces (for bite-size flatbreads). Roll each piece into a circle, flatten it with the heel of your hand and then roll into a thin disc with a rolling pin. Put the discs on a baking tray and spread the lamb mixture over the top. Bake for 15 minutes, or until crisp and golden.

Remove from the oven and serve topped with the pine kernels, micro mint and pomegranate seeds. Drizzle with a little more pomegranate molasses before serving, if you like.

Chorizo, Sweet Potato & Coriander Quesadillas

PREPARATION TIME: 20 minutes | COOKING TIME: 1 hour 35 minutes | SERVES: 6

200g/7oz sweet potatoes
150g/5½oz uncooked chorizo
1 red onion, roughly chopped
1 red chilli, deseeded and finely chopped
100g/3½oz feta cheese
1 small handful of coriander leaves, plus extra to serve
6 flour tortillas

TO SERVE
100g/3½oz pickled jalepeño chillies
100g/3½oz/generous ⅓ cup soured cream
1 lime, cut into wedges

Quesadillas are wonderful to make for last-minute nibbles as they are so versatile. You can stuff them with all sorts of fillings, including the spicy and delicious combination I have used here.

Put the sweet potatoes in a saucepan of boiling water, reduce the heat to low and simmer, covered, for 20 minutes until cooked through. Be very careful not to overcook, as sweet potato retains a lot of water. Drain the sweet potatoes in a colander and leave to one side to cool, uncovered, then cut into small dice.

Heat a frying pan over a medium-high heat. Crumble in the chorizo and cook, stirring frequently, for 4 minutes until the oil is released. Add the onion and chilli and cook, stirring occasionally, for 8 minutes until browned. Add the diced sweet potato, feta and coriander, toss well and then remove from the heat.

Preheat the oven to 160°C/325°F/Gas 3. Put three baking sheets or tins in the oven to warm. Lay one tortilla flat on a chopping board. Spread one-sixth of the chorizo and potato mixture over half the tortilla and then fold over the other half to make one quesadilla. Repeat with the remaining tortillas and chorizo and potato mixture. Heat a large frying pan or ridged griddle pan over a medium heat. Lay a quesadilla in the pan and cook for 5 minutes on each side until crisp and golden. Remove from the pan and put at one end of one of the baking sheets to keep warm in the oven while you cook the remaining quesadillas, adding them in turn to the baking sheets.

Cut the quesadillas in half, put on a platter and sprinkle over some extra coriander. Serve immediately with the pickled jalepeños, soured cream and lime wedges.

Vietnamese Beef Spring Rolls

PREPARATION TIME: 25 minutes, plus 1 hour marinating time and making the sauce | COOKING TIME: 8 minutes | SERVES: 4

300g/10½oz beef steak, ideally beef sirloin
100g/3½oz fine vermicelli rice noodles
a drizzle of sesame oil
1 small handful of micro mint leaves or roughly chopped mint leaves
1 small handful of micro coriander leaves or roughly chopped coriander leaves
8 rice paper wrappers
½ cucumber, cut into matchsticks
1 carrot, peeled and cut into matchsticks
sea salt and freshly ground black pepper

MARINADE
2 garlic cloves, finely chopped
1 lemongrass stalk, outer leaves removed, end cut off and bruised
zest of 1 lime
1 chilli, finely chopped
1 tsp brown sugar
1 tbsp dry sherry

TO SERVE
Dipping Sauce
   (see page 198)

These light and fresh spring rolls are great instead of the sludgy deep-fried version. Use king prawns or cooked chicken strips for a change if you don't feel like beef.

To make the marinade, mix all the ingredients together in a large bowl. Add the steak, then spoon over the marinade. Cover with clear film and leave to marinate in the fridge for 1 hour.

Put the noodles into a bowl and cover with boiling water. Leave to sit for 5 minutes, then drain in a colander and refresh under cold water. Return the noodles to the bowl and toss with the sesame oil.

Heat a frying pan over a medium-high heat. Pat dry the steaks with kitchen paper, then season with salt and pepper. Put the steaks in the hot pan and sear for 4 minutes on each side until seared but still pink and juicy inside. Remove from the heat and leave to rest on a plate for 5 minutes, then cut into thin slices. Meanwhile, stir the micro mint and micro coriander into the dipping sauce, reserving a large pinch of each to serve.

Pour some hot water into a deep saucer or soup bowl. Taking one rice paper wrapper at a time, soak the sheet in the water until softened. Remove, shake off any excess water, and lay flat on a chopping board. Leaving a 1cm/½in edge at each end, arrange horizontally along the middle of the rice paper: a good pinch each of the noodles, cucumber and carrot and a few slices of beef. Fold over the ends and then roll up tightly. Put on a plate, cover with a tea towel and make up the remaining spring rolls. Serve sprinkled with the reserved micro herbs and with the dipping sauce on the side.

Asian Beef Carpaccio with Micro Herbs

PREPARATION TIME: 15 minutes, plus minimum 30 minutes chilling time | COOKING TIME: 15 minutes | SERVES: 4

400g/14oz beef fillet
150ml/5fl oz/scant ⅔ cup
   vegetable oil
8 garlic cloves, finely
   sliced lengthways
1 small handful of micro
   coriander
1 small handful of micro
   Thai purple basil
sea salt and freshly
   ground pepper

DRESSING
2 tbsp soy sauce
½ tsp caster sugar
1 red chilli, deseeded and
   finely chopped
½ tsp sesame oil

This is my version of a carpaccio: slightly rustic and lightly seared on the outside, with crunchy garlic crisps and a sweet, salty and lightly spiced dressing. The garlic crisps are brilliant and the flavours work well, especially the unique aniseed tones of the Thai purple basil.

Heat a non-stick frying pan over a high heat until smoking hot and season the beef well with salt and pepper. Put the beef in the pan and sear all round until well seared and a crust forms. This will take 8–10 minutes. Remove from the pan and leave to cool.

When the beef has cooled (it doesn't need to be cold), roll it several times in clear film as tightly as possible to create a sausage shape. Tie at both ends and put in the fridge for 30 minutes to 1 hour. Meanwhile, whisk all the dressing ingredients together in a small bowl until thoroughly combined.

Heat the vegetable oil in a heavy-based saucepan over a medium heat until hot. Test by dropping in a slice of garlic, which should sizzle. Add the garlic slices in batches, so they have plenty of space around them, and cook until a light golden brown. Keep a close eye on the garlic, as it will cook quickly and will burn easily. Using a slotted spoon, remove from the oil and drain on kitchen paper.

When you are ready to eat, remove the beef from the fridge and slice it very thinly. Serve overlapping slices sprinkled with the micro coriander, micro Thai purple basil and garlic crisps and drizzled with the dressing.

Sesame Tuna with Pink Grapefruit Salad & Wasabi Potato Salad

PREPARATION TIME: 20 minutes, plus making the mayonnaise | COOKING TIME: 25 minutes | SERVES: 4

1 tbsp sesame seeds
4 thick tuna steaks, about
   175g/6oz each
400g/14oz new potatoes
1 tbsp Mayonnaise
   (see page 199)
1 tsp wasabi paste
1 pink grapefruit
1 tbsp light soy sauce
1 tsp sesame oil
1 tsp groundnut oil, plus
   extra for frying
50g/1¾oz mizuna, plus
   extra for scattering
1 tbsp micro shiso cress,
   plus extra for scattering

When I started developing this recipe I wasn't sure whether it would come out as I was hoping. In fact it did – and the seared pink tuna, hot creamy wasabi and pink grapefuit are excellent together. It's a fusion dish I suppose, especially if you can find Japanese mayonnaise.

Sprinkle the sesame seeds onto a plate and press both sides of each tuna steak into them. Move the steaks to a clean plate, cover with clear film and put in the fridge.

Put the potatoes in a large saucepan, cover with water and bring to the boil. Turn the heat down and simmer, covered, for 15 minutes, or until cooked through. Drain the potatoes in a colander and leave to one side to cool.

Mix the mayonnaise and wasabi together in a large bowl. Rub the skins off the potatoes and cut the flesh into small cubes. Add the potatoes to the mayonnaise, mix and toss until well coated. Leave to one side.

Using a sharp knife, peel the grapefruit, removing all the skin and pith, then carefully cut into segments over a bowl so any juice is caught. Add the soy sauce and the sesame and groundnut oils to the bowl with the juices and segments and mix together until well combined. Add the mizuna and micro cress and toss again.

Heat a splash of groundnut oil in a large frying pan over a medium heat. Add the tuna and sear on both sides for 4 minutes, or until seared but still pink inside. Serve the seared tuna with the wasabi potato salad and the pink grapefruit salad, scattered with extra mizuna and micro shiso cress.

Sardines Wrapped in Vine Leaves with Verjuice-Poached Grapes

PREPARATION TIME: 20 minutes | COOKING TIME: 30 minutes | SERVES: 4

8 bottled vine leaves
8 plump sardines, gutted
    and heads removed

POACHED GRAPES
3 tbsp verjuice or
    white wine
2 tsp caster sugar
300g/10½oz white
    seedless grapes

HERB CROSTINI
8 small slices of rustic
    French bread, cut on
    the diagonal
1 tbsp finely chopped
    flat-leaf parsely
1 tsp finely chopped
    tarragon
3 tbsp extra virgin
    olive oil
1 tsp lemon zest
sea salt

I love cooking sardines wrapped in vine leaves as they keep in more of the moisture and add flavour. I have added a slightly sour aspect with the verjuice-poached grapes, and chosen some herb crostini for some crunch.

To make the poached grapes, put the verjuice, sugar and 150ml/5fl oz/scant ⅔ cup water into a saucepan, bring to the boil and then simmer for 10 minutes. Add the grapes to the pan and simmer for a further 10 minutes, then take off the heat.

To make the herb crostini, heat the grill until hot, then toast the slices of bread on each side until crisp. Mix the parsely, tarragon, olive oil and lemon zest together in a small dish, then season with salt. Spread a little on each slice of bread.

Wrap a vine leaf around each sardine and fry in a large frying pan over a medium heat for 4–6 minutes on each side until just cooked through. Serve the sardines with the grapes and herb crostini.

"The verjuice-poached grapes balance the oiliness of the sardines perfectly."

Sea Bass Sashimi with Pomegranate & Micro Herbs

PREPARATION TIME: 20 minutes | SERVES: 4

4 very fresh sea bass
  fillets, skins on, about
  200g/7oz total weight
100g/3½oz pomegranate
  seeds or the seeds
  tapped out of
  1 pomegranate
1 small handful of mixed
  micro herbs
1 small handful of radish
  sprouts
sea salt and freshly
  ground black pepper

LEMON DRESSING
juice of 1 lemon
3 generous tbsp extra
  virgin olive oil

You need super-fresh fish for this Beirut Beach Club-inspired dish, and the sourness of the pomegranate really works well with it. It's a very quick dish, designed to be eaten straight away.

Lay the sea bass, skin-side down, on a chopping board. The board needs to be secure, so put it on a dampened tea towel, if necessary. Using a sharp knife, carefully cut off thin slices of fish on a diagonal. Lay the slices on a separate chopping board or plate, cover with clear film and put in the fridge while you make the dressing.

Mix the lemon dressing ingredients together in a small bowl and season with salt and pepper.

Arrange the sea bass slices on each plate in a pretty and decorative way. Sprinkle over the pomegranate seeds, drizzle over the lemon dressing and then arrange the micro herbs and radish sprouts in the middle. Serve immediately.

Prawn Ceviche

PREPARATION TIME: 15 minutes, plus 1 hour marinating time | COOKING TIME: 10 minutes | SERVES: 4

400g/14oz peeled,
  cooked king prawns
100g/3½oz cherry
  tomatoes, quartered
1 red onion, finely
  chopped
1 red pepper, deseeded
  and finely diced
1 tbsp finely chopped
  pickled jalapeño chilli
1 heaped tbsp roughly
  chopped coriander
  leaves
juice of 1 lime
juice of ½ lemon
2 sweetcorn cobs, kernels
  sliced off

TO SERVE
100g/3½oz tortilla chips

Ceviche is traditionally fresh raw fish marinated in citrus juice. My version is a twist on this to make a modern type of prawn cocktail. You can serve it in little glass dishes and use the tortilla chips to scoop up the juicy prawns. Blue corn chips look visually stunning.

Slice the king prawns in half down the middle and put in a large bowl. Add the cherry tomatoes, onion, red pepper, jalapeño chilli, coriander and the lime and lemon juices, and toss until well combined.

Heat the grill until very hot. Spread the sweetcorn kernels on a baking tray and put under the grill for 10 minutes, or until they are slightly charred, stirring occasionally. Remove the tray from the grill and leave the corn to cool, then stir into the prawn and vegetable mixture. Cover the bowl with clear film and marinate in the fridge for 1 hour. Serve with the tortilla chips.

Potted Shrimp & Samphire Tarts

PREPARATION TIME: **30 minutes, plus 30 minutes resting time** | COOKING TIME: **50 minutes** | MAKES: **4 tarts**

250g/9oz butter, chilled
and roughly diced
500g/1lb 2oz/4 cups
plain flour, plus extra
for dusting
1 tsp olive oil
2 banana shallots,
finely diced
200g/7oz potted shrimps
or peeled brown
shrimps
2 eggs
3 tbsp double cream
¼ tsp ground mace
100g/3½oz samphire or
fine asparagus
sea salt and freshly
ground black pepper

TO SERVE
mixed salad leaves

Blitz the butter and flour in a blender or food processor until they resemble fine breadcrumbs. With the motor running, gradually add 3–4 tablespoons iced cold water until you get a smooth dough – you don't want it too wet. Turn the dough out onto a lightly floured surface and shape into a ball, then wrap in clear film and put in the fridge for 30 minutes.

Preheat the oven to 180°C/350°F/Gas 4. Roll out the pastry on a lightly floured surface until 3mm/⅛in thick. Using a round pastry cutter, about 14cm/5½in in diameter, or a saucer of similar size and a sharp knife, cut out 4 discs and use them to line four 9cm/3½in tart tins. (There will be some leftover pastry: wrap in clear film and freeze for another day.) Line each one with baking parchment and weight the paper down with pastry weights or rice. Bake in the oven for 15 minutes, then remove the weights and paper, prick the base with a fork and bake for a further 5 minutes until the pastry is just starting to turn golden.

Meanwhile, heat the oil in a frying pan over a medium-low heat, then add the shallots and fry gently for about 5 minutes, or until softened and translucent. Add the potted shrimps and stir-fry for 1–2 minutes until warmed through, then leave to one side, draining off the excess oil first. (If you are using brown shrimps, this does not apply.)

Whisk the eggs and cream together in a bowl until well combined. Add the mace and season with salt and pepper, then add the shrimps and stir well.

Put the tart tins on a baking sheet and carefully pour the egg and shrimp mixture into the tart cases, making sure the shrimps are equally divided into the cases. Nestle the samphire into the filling. (If using asparagus, trim the spears as required to fit neatly.)

Put in the oven and bake for 20 minutes, or until just set and golden. Remove from the oven and serve either hot or warm with mixed salad leaves.

"This is a new way to use potted shrimps. The samphire adds another layer of seaside flavours."

Beetroot-Cured Salmon Gravlax

PREPARATION TIME: 25 minutes, plus 24 hours curing time | SERVES: 4 (plus a little extra)

800g/1lb 12oz side of
   salmon, skin on
150g/5½oz sea salt
100g/3½oz/scant ½ cup
   brown sugar
zest of 1 lemon
1 tsp freshly ground black
   pepper
200g/7oz raw beetroot,
   peeled and grated
1 small handful of
   tarragon leaves, roughly
   chopped
1 small handful of edible
   micro flowers, such as
   borage, pansies and
   chive flowers, to scatter

DRESSING
1 tbsp horseradish
1 tbsp wholegrain
   mustard
1 tsp white wine vinegar
2 tsp caster sugar
sea salt and freshly
   ground black pepper

TO SERVE
blinis, rye bread or Oaty
   Soda Bread (see page
   181), (optional)

This dish fulfils my love of pretty colours, delicate flavours and simple but impressive techniques. Curing salmon is one of those processes that sounds so much harder and more time consuming than it actually is, and it knocks people's socks off! The beetroot adds amazing colourful edges.

Check the salmon for pin bones and remove, then trim off any excess fatty bits from the edges of the salmon.

Mix the salt, sugar, lemon zest and pepper together in a small bowl. Put the fish, skin-side down, on a plastic tray and pat the salt mixture on top in an even layer. Spread the grated beetroot over the salt mixture, then cover with clear film and put a second tray or chopping board on top of the salmon. Put weights on the tray such as cans of food, then put in the fridge to cure for at least 24 hours.

Whisk all the ingredients for the dressing together with 2 teaspoons water until thoroughly combined, then cover and put in the fridge with the salmon.

Scrape the beetroot and salt mixture off the salmon and discard. Quickly wash the salmon under cold water and pat dry with kitchen paper. Put the salmon on a chopping board and, using a very sharp knife, cut it on the diagonal into thin slices. Use the skin to hold onto as you cut to keep the fish steady, and discard it when you have finished cutting the fish.

Drizzle the dressing over the salmon, then scatter over the tarragon and edible flowers. Serve with blinis, rye bread or soda bread, if you like.

Hot & Sour Prawn Salad

PREPARATION TIME: 20 minutes | COOKING TIME: 2 minutes | SERVES: 4

200g/7oz mangetout
100g/3½oz bean sprouts
100g/3½oz pea shoots
2 carrots, peeled and cut
  into thin strips with a
  swivel-bladed peeler
400g/14oz peeled,
  cooked king prawns
1 small handful of
  coriander leaves,
  roughly chopped,
  for sprinkling

HOT & SOUR DRESSING
1 tbsp peanuts
1 red chilli
a pinch of caster sugar
a pinch of chilli powder
  or dried flakes
1 tsp fish sauce
1 tsp lime juice
1 tsp rice wine vinegar
1 tsp soy sauce

Thai and South East Asian cooking is all about balance of flavours. Sweet, salty, hot and sour: they all need to be combined in the perfect ratio. Test as you go along and adapt to your own tastes. You can serve this as a starter followed by the Beef Rendang (see page 110) or the Pad Thai (see page 128).

To make the hot and sour dressing, put the peanuts, chilli and sugar in a small blender and grind to a smooth paste, or use a mortar and pestle. Scrape the paste into a small bowl and mix together with the remaining dressing ingredients until well combined.

Bring a saucepan of water to the boil and add the mangetout. Boil for just 2 minutes, then drain and refresh under cold water to stop the cooking process, then drain thoroughly again. Tip the peas into a large bowl and toss together with the bean sprouts, pea shoots, carrots and prawns. Pour the dressing over the salad and stir well.

This salad can be made up to 1 hour before serving with the coriander sprinkled over the top.

Five-Spice Scallops with Fennel Purée & Orange Dressing

PREPARATION TIME: 20 minutes | COOKING TIME: 25 minutes | SERVES: 4

2 tsp Chinese five-spice
    powder
12 diver-caught scallops,
    corals removed
1 tsp olive oil
sea salt and freshly
    ground black pepper
1 small handful of cress,
    to sprinkle

FENNEL PURÉE
2 heads of fennel,
    trimmed and roughly
    chopped
25g/1oz butter
400ml/14fl oz/generous
    1½ cups vegetable
    stock
1 tbsp crème fraîche

ORANGE DRESSING
1 orange
2 tsp light soy sauce
3 tsp light olive oil

Scallops are one of nature's wonders: the sweet soft meat with a good caramelized outside is unbeaten for perfect seafood. I have paired them with a fennel purée, and the aniseed flavours are heightened by the star anise in the five-spice powder.

To make the fennel purée, put the fennel, butter and stock in a saucepan over a high heat and bring to the boil. Reduce the heat to low, then simmer for 20 minutes, or until the fennel is softened. Drain the fennel, reserving 1 tablespoon of the stock, then tip the fennel and stock into a food processor or blender and blitz to a fine purée. Season with salt and pepper, add the crème fraîche and blitz again briefly to combine. Leave to one side.

To make the dressing, using a sharp knife, peel the orange, removing all the skin and pith, then carefully cut into segments over a bowl so any juice is caught. Cut the segments into slightly smaller pieces, then mix together with the soy sauce and oil in the bowl until well combined. Leave to one side.

Sprinkle the Chinese five-spice powder onto a plate. Pat the scallops dry with kitchen paper, then press both sides of each of the scallops into the powder and season them with salt.

Heat a frying pan over a high heat and add the oil. Keeping the heat high, add the scallops and fry for about 2½ minutes on each side until golden brown but still tender.

Put the scallops on top of the fennel purée, then sprinkle over the cress and drizzle over the dressing. Serve immediately.

Crab, Ginger & Coconut Pancakes

PREPARATION TIME: 15 minutes, plus 30 minutes resting time | COOKING TIME: 35 minutes | SERVES: 4

1–2 tsp groundnut oil
1 tsp sesame oil
2.5cm/1in piece of root ginger, peeled and finely chopped
300g/10½oz picked cooked white crab meat
1 tsp soy sauce

PANCAKE BATTER
175g/6oz/heaped 1 cup rice flour
250ml/9fl oz/1 cup coconut milk
1 tsp turmeric
1 tbsp snipped chives, plus extra for sprinkling
a pinch of sea salt

TO SERVE
2 tbsp oyster sauce

When I make these, I am trying to recreate a dish I had in Malaysia. You can use strips of pork in the mixture, or sometimes I add fresh herbs, prawns and peanuts.

To make the pancake batter, whisk together the rice flour, coconut milk, turmeric, chives and sea salt in a bowl with 125ml/4fl oz/½ cup water until thoroughly combined. Cover with clear film and leave to rest in the fridge for 30 minutes.

To cook the pancakes, preheat the oven to 140°C/275°F/Gas 1 and heat a frying pan with a base about 20cm/8in in diameter over a medium-high heat. Add some of the groundnut oil, and, when it is hot, pour in one-quarter of the pancake batter. Tilt the pan to spread the batter into a thin, lacy layer, then cook the pancake for 5 minutes until the batter is set and the edges are starting to turn golden. Flip the pancake over and cook for a further 2–3 minutes until golden. Turn the pancake out onto a heatproof serving plate and keep warm in the oven while you cook the remaining 3 pancakes, adding more oil to the pan as required.

Heat the sesame oil in a frying pan over a medium heat, then add the ginger and cook, stirring often, for 2 minutes. Add the crab meat and soy sauce and stir-fry until heated through. Divide the crab mixture onto the pancakes and roll them up. Serve immediately with the oyster sauce drizzled over and sprinkled with chives.

"I love the coconut- and turmeric-flavoured batter and the flavoursome filling in these pancakes. "

Tomato & Geranium Jellies with Crab & Micro Basil

PREPARATION TIME: 20 minutes, plus overnight straining time and 4 hours setting time | COOKING TIME: 2 minutes | SERVES: 4

2kg/4lb 8oz ripe tomatoes
1 small handful of basil
100ml/3½fl oz/scant ½ cup white balsamic vinegar
100ml/3½fl oz/scant ½ cup spring water
2 tsp caster sugar
1 tsp sea salt
3 geranium leaves
10 gelatine sheets
300g/10½oz cooked white crab meat
olive oil, for dressing
8 yellow cherry tomatoes, halved
8 red cherry tomatoes, halved

TO SERVE
1 small handful of micro purple basil

Although this may seem like a strange combination, tomatoes and geranium contain a similar chemical compound and so they really bring out the best in each other. This is a delicate jelly made from the essence of tomato, then topped with a little crab. Perfect for a light summer dish.

Put the tomatoes, basil, white balsamic vinegar, spring water, caster sugar, sea salt and geranium leaves in a blender or food processor and blitz until finely chopped. Line a colander with a dampened piece of muslin, then rest the colander over a large bowl so that it hangs with plenty of space in the bowl below it. Pour the tomato mix into the colander, cover with clear film and put in the fridge overnight for the juices to collect in the bowl.

The next day, gently squeeze out the remaining juice from the tomato mix. Don't over-squeeze, as you don't want any of the pulp, which will make the liquid cloudy. You need about 750ml/26fl oz/3 cups liquid. If there is less, don't dilute it – change the ingredient measurements to 500ml/17fl oz/2 cups liquid and 7 gelatine sheets.

Heat 200ml/7fl oz/generous ¾ cup of the tomato liquid in a saucepan until just boiling, then remove from the heat. Meanwhile, soak the gelatine sheets in some cold water for about 5 minutes until softened, then squeeze to remove any excess water and stir into the heated tomato liquid until dissolved. Pour the tomato mix into the remaining tomato liquid, then divide it between four soup bowls. Put in the fridge, uncovered, for 3–4 hours to set.

When you are ready to eat, dress the crab in a little olive oil. Pile the crab onto the jellies, add the tomatoes and sprinkle over the micro basil to serve.

Lobster Rolls with Pea Shoots

PREPARATION TIME: 40 minutes, plus 1 hour freezing time and making the rolls and mayonnaise | COOKING TIME: 6 minutes | SERVES: 4

2 live lobsters each weighing 500g/1lb 2oz; or 600g/1lb 5oz cooked lobster meat
4 hot dog rolls made using the Deluxe Burger Buns recipe (see page 201)
Mayonnaise (see page 199)
sea salt and freshly ground black pepper

These decadent rolls have a New England vibe to them and are perfect with a crisp white wine. You could make them with prawns too: just as good but far cheaper. Serve with hot dog rolls made with my buttery sweet dough or use toasted bought brioche rolls.

If using live lobsters, put them in the freezer for up to 1 hour before cooking. This is considered to be one of the kindest and most humane methods to cook lobsters, as it either kills them or desensitizes them so that they don't feel pain.

Bring a large saucepan of water to the boil, then add the lobsters and cook until the shells turn red. The cooking time will depend on the size of the lobsters, but the general rule is 10 minutes per 450g/1lb. So, if you decide to use one larger lobster, calculate the cooking time accordingly. Remove the lobsters from the water and put on a tray to cool.

To remove the meat from the lobsters, take a large knife and insert the tip between the eyes of one of the lobsters, then draw the knife along the middle to cut it in half. Remove the tail meat and any extra little bits in the body. Pull off the claw and legs, crack them with a meat mallet or a large knife and remove the meat. Repeat this process with the second lobster, then chop all the meat into small pieces, put it in a bowl and season with salt and pepper, adding mayonnaise to taste.

Cut each roll along the middle lengthways, keeping a "hinge" at the back. Spoon the lobster mixture into the rolls, then serve. If you want to make the mixture in advance, cover with clear film and put in the fridge to chill until you are ready to serve the rolls.

Halloumi, Quinoa, Pomegranate & Mint Salad

PREPARATION TIME: 10 minutes, plus making the sauce | COOKING TIME: 30 minutes | SERVES: 4

200g/7oz/1 cup quinoa
4 spring onions, finely
   sliced
200g/7oz pink radishes,
   finely sliced
1 large handful of mint
   leaves, roughly chopped
50g/1¾oz nibbed
   pistachios or chopped
   pistachios
50g/1¾oz/heaped ¼ cup
   pomegranate seeds
300g/10½oz halloumi
   cheese

DRESSING
juice of 1 lemon
generous 3 tbsp olive oil
2 tbsp pomegranate
   molasses

TO SERVE
Yogurt Sauce (see page
   199) (optional)

I love the Middle Eastern flavours of pomegranate, pistachios and mint, combined here with halloumi cheese. I have added quinoa, rather than the traditional bulgar wheat or couscous, to make it a more protein-based dish. The result is a jewel-like salad.

Pour the quinoa into a saucepan and cook according to the packet instructions. It is cooked just like rice, with the lid on and until the water is absorbed, and should take about 20 minutes. Leave to cool.

Meanwhile, to make the dressing, whisk together all the ingredients until thoroughly combined. Leave to one side.

Tip the quinoa into a large mixing bowl. Add the spring onions and radishes and mix to combine, then add the mint, pistachios, pomegranate seeds and dressing and toss until well combined. The salad can be made a few hours in advance, if you like, as it will allow the flavours to develop.

When you are ready to eat, heat a ridged griddle pan over a medium-high heat. Slice the halloumi into 1cm/½in slices and chargrill on each side for 3 minutes, or until soft and well marked with charred lines.

Serve the halloumi on top of piles of the quinoa salad, with the yogurt sauce on the side, if you like.

Superfood Salad with Avocado & Lemon Dressings

PREPARATION TIME: **15 minutes** | COOKING TIME: **5 minutes** | SERVES: **4**

200g/7oz asparagus, trimmed

100g/3½oz mixed micro lettuce leaves

2 heads of fennel, very finely sliced

2 carrots, peeled and grated

150g/5½oz cooked beetroot, peeled and diced

Cooked Turkey (see page 205) (optional)

50g/1¾oz pomegranate seeds or the seeds tapped out of ½ pomegranate

25g/1oz/scant ¼ cup macadamia nuts, chopped

AVOCADO DRESSING

2 ripe avocadoes

½ garlic clove, finely chopped

1 tsp olive oil

1 tbsp natural yogurt

juice of 1 lemon

sea salt and freshly ground black pepper

LEMON DRESSING

juice of 2 lemons

5 tbsp olive oil

Liver-boosting beetroot, cleansing asparagus and iron-rich micro leaves, plus a dressing with the good fats of avocado and good bacteria of yogurt and olive oil. All topped off with crunchy macadamia nuts. What could be healthier?

Bring a pan of water to the boil and blanch the asparagus for 4–6 minutes until just cooked. Drain and refresh under cold water to stop the cooking process.

While the asparagus is cooking, make the avocado dressing by putting all the ingredients in a blender or food processor with 5 teaspoons water, blitzing until smooth then seasoning with salt and pepper. Also make the lemon dressing by whisking together the lemon juice and olive oil in a small bowl until thoroughly combined.

To assemble the salad you will need a large platter. Layer the micro lettuce leaves over the platter, then layer the fennel, carrots, beetroot, asparagus and finally the shredded turkey on top, if using. Pour the avocado dressing over the salad and sprinkle over the pomegranate seeds and macadamia nuts. Serve with the lemon dressing on the side.

Cauliflower & Onion Pakoras
with Mango & Fenugreek Salsa

PREPARATION TIME: 25 minutes, plus 15 minutes resting time | COOKING TIME: 30 minutes | SERVES: 4

300g/10½oz cauliflower
  florets
300ml/10½fl oz/scant
  1¼ cups vegetable oil
2 red onions, sliced into
  thick rings

MANGO & FENUGREEK
SALSA
2 mangoes
1 shallot, finely diced
1 red chilli, deseeded and
  finely diced
½ tsp fenugreek seeds
3 tablespoons white wine
  vinegar
25g/1oz brown sugar
1 tsp chopped coriander
  leaves

BATTER
250g/9oz/2¼ cup
  gram flour
1 tsp cumin seeds
½ tsp turmeric
½ tsp garam masala
juice of 1 lemon
salt and freshly ground
  black pepper

These onion rings and cauliflower florets, coated in a spicy crisp gram flour batter, are very moreish. The salsa is a modern touch to add freshness to the dish.

To make the mango and fenugreek salsa, carefully slice each mango down both sides, using a sharp knife, avoiding the stone. On the inside of each slice, cut the flesh into squares, cutting down to the peel but not piercing it, and scoop out with a spoon. Peel the remaining parts of the mango and slice the flesh from the stone. Put the mango in a saucepan over a medium-high heat with all the other salsa ingredients except the coriander, and bring to the boil. Reduce the heat to low and simmer for 20 minutes until soft and fragrant. Remove from the heat and leave to cool, then stir in the coriander.

Meanwhile, to make the batter, mix the gram flour, spices and lemon juice together in a bowl until well combined, then add 300ml/10½fl oz/scant 1¼ cups water and beat until the batter is smooth and thick. Season with salt and pepper, then cover with clear film and rest in the fridge for 15 minutes.

While the batter is resting, bring a large saucepan of water to the boil and blanch the cauliflower for 3 minutes. Drain in a colander and refresh under cold water. Leave to one side to drain completely.

Heat the oil in a large, heavy-based saucepan over a medium heat until hot – but be very careful not to overheat the oil. It will be hot enough when an onion ring dropped into the oil sizzles.

When you are ready to eat, quickly dip half the blanched cauliflower and onion rings in the batter, a piece at a time, and slide into the oil. Deep-fry for a few minutes until golden and crisp, then scoop out of the oil using a slotted spoon and drain on kitchen paper. Repeat with the remaining vegetables. (It is important not to cook too many pieces at the same time, as the oil temperature will drop.) Serve the pakoras with the salsa on the side.

Courgette, Mozzarella & Basil Bruschetta

PREPARATION TIME: 10 minutes | COOKING TIME: 10 minutes | SERVES: 4

4 courgettes
1 tbsp olive oil, plus extra
    for drizzling
½ tsp chilli flakes
1 tsp lemon zest
4 slices of sourdough
    bread
1 large garlic clove, halved
2 balls of buffalo
    mozzarella cheese
1 small handful of basil
    leaves
sea salt and freshly
    ground black pepper

Sometimes simple is good. Use the best mozzarella and the freshest courgettes you can find for the topping, and good-quality bread finished off with the richest olive oil for the base. I love these as a light lunch or as pre-dinner nibbles with drinks.

Slice the courgettes lengthways into thin ribbons using a swivel-bladed vegetable peeler. Heat the oil in a large frying pan over a medium heat, then add the courgettes and chilli flakes, season with salt and pepper and fry, stirring occasionally, for about 10 minutes until softened. Stir through the lemon zest and remove from the heat.

Meanwhile, heat the grill and chargrill the sourdough slices or toast them in a toaster. Rub the garlic, cut-side down, over one side of each slice.

Pile the courgette ribbons on top of the sourdough slices, then tear up the mozzarella and put it on the courgette. Sprinkle over the basil leaves and drizzle over a little oil. Serve immediately.

Roasted Portabello Mushroom & Garlic Cream Cheese Focaccias

PREPARATION TIME: 10 minutes | COOKING TIME: 25 minutes | SERVES: 4

4 tomatoes
4 Portabello or other large field mushrooms, trimmed and peeled
4 garlic cloves
1 thyme sprig, leaves picked, plus extra for sprinkling
1 tbsp olive oil
4 squares of focaccia, about 10 x 10cm/ 4 x 4in, or 4 mini focaccia rolls
150g/5½oz garlic and herb cream cheese
sea salt and freshly ground black pepper

Vegetarians rejoice! The hot, juicy, meaty mushroom melts the garlic cream cheese, which is then balanced by the acidity of the roasted tomatoes. You can use any bread, but I like mini focaccia rolls best.

Preheat the oven to 200°C/400°F/Gas 6. Slice off the top and bottom from each tomato, then cut the tomatoes into thick slices, widthways. Lay the mushrooms in a baking tray, season with salt and pepper and then top each mushroom with a few slices of tomato. Crush the garlic cloves with the flat edge of a large knife and put 1 clove on each of the mushrooms. Sprinkle over the thyme, season again and drizzle over the oil.

Put in the oven and roast for 15–20 minutes until the mushrooms are juicy and cooked through. Turn off the oven, leaving the tray there to keep the mushrooms warm.

Slice the focaccia squares in half and toast the insides under a hot grill. Spread each half with a thick layer of the cream cheese, then remove the tray of mushrooms from the oven and put a roasted mushroom on each of the bottom halves, removing the garlic cloves, if you like. Sprinkle with thyme, then sandwich the focaccia squares together and serve.

Beetroot Mousse with Creamy Goat's Cheese

PREPARATION TIME: 20 minutes, plus overnight chilling time | COOKING TIME: 30 minutes | SERVES: 4

1 red onion, roughly
  chopped
400g/14oz raw beetroot,
  peeled and quartered
1 garlic clove
6 tbsp olive oil
1 tsp caster sugar
4 gelatine sheets
250ml/9fl oz/1 cup hot
  vegetable stock
1 tbsp lemon juice
2 large egg whites
200g/7oz soft, rindless
  goat's cheese
50ml/2fl oz/scant ¼ cup
  double cream
sea salt and freshly
  ground black pepper

TO SERVE
2 handfuls of red
  beetroot sprouts
toast triangles

Beetroot is a wonderful vegetable: it's colour, texture and flavour are great and it's also a healthy vegetable with liver-cleansing properties. Here I have made a brightly coloured and deeply flavoured beetroot mousse, which is great spread on toast.

Preheat the oven to 200°C/400°F/Gas 6. Put the onion, beetroot and garlic on a baking tray, drizzle the oil over and season with the sugar, salt and pepper. Cover with foil and cook for 30 minutes until tender.

Soak the gelatine sheets in cold water for about 5 minutes until softened, then squeeze to remove any excess water and put in a heatproof jug with the hot stock and stir until dissolved. Leave to cool, then put the roasted beetroot, onion, garlic and lemon juice in a blender or food processor and pour in the stock. Blitz until very fine, then check the seasoning.

Whisk the egg whites in a large, clean bowl until soft peaks form, then, using a metal spoon, fold the egg whites into the beetroot mixture. Spoon the mousse into serving bowls and put in the fridge to set overnight.

Just before serving, mix the goat's cheese with the cream and spoon on top of each beetroot mousse. Sprinkle the red beetroot sprouts over the top and serve toast triangles on the side.

Twice-Baked Cheese Soufflés with Tomato & Micro Basil Salad

PREPARATION TIME: 25 minutes, plus 10 minutes infusing time and 10 minutes chilling time |
COOKING TIME: 35 minutes | SERVES: 4

250ml/9fl oz/1 cup milk
1 onion, finely chopped
140g/5oz butter
50g/1¾oz/scant ½ cup
   plain flour
200g/7oz mature
   Cheddar cheese, grated
1 tsp English mustard
1 tsp wholegrain mustard
3 large eggs, separated
150ml/5fl oz/scant ⅔ cup
   double cream
50g/1¾oz Parmesan
   cheese, finely grated
sea salt and freshly
   ground black pepper

TOMATO & MICRO BASIL
SALAD
100g/3½oz cherry
   tomatoes, quartered
5 tsp white balsamic
   vinegar
a pinch of caster sugar
1 large handful of
   micro basil

Put the milk and onion in a saucepan over a medium heat and bring slowly to the boil. Turn off the heat immediately and leave to infuse for 10 minutes. Meanwhile, melt 100g/3½oz of the butter and brush four 150ml/5fl oz/scant ⅔ cup ramekins with the butter in a lovely thick layer. Chill the ramekins in the fridge, then line with another layer of butter. Repeat until all the butter is used.

Strain the milk through a fine sieve into a jug. Melt the remaining butter in a non-stick saucepan, add in the flour and cook, stirring continuously with a wooden spoon, for 1 minute. Gradually whisk in the milk until smooth. Add the Cheddar cheese and mustard, then remove from the heat and whisk in the egg yolks, one at a time. Season with salt and pepper and leave to one side to cool.

Preheat the oven to 180°C/350°F/Gas 4. When the cheese mixture is cool, whisk the egg whites in a large, clean bowl with a hand-held electric beater until stiff peaks form. Tip the egg whites into the cheese mixture and gently fold in with a metal spoon. Stir the mixture as little as possible to retain the air.

Put the prepared ramekins in a roasting dish and divide the soufflé mixture between them. Pour boiling water into the roasting dish until it comes two-thirds of the way up the sides of the ramekins, then put the dish in the oven. Bake the soufflés for 15 minutes until risen and golden brown. Remove the dish from the oven and the ramekins from the water bath and leave to cool completely – they will collapse. Increase the oven temperature to 200°C/400°F/Gas 6.

Turn out the collapsed soufflés into four small ovenproof dishes. Pour the cream over the top of the soufflés and sprinkle with the Parmesan. Bake for 15 minutes, or until golden and crispy. Meanwhile, make the tomato and micro basil salad by tossing together all the ingredients in a bowl until well combined. Serve the soufflés immediately with the salad.

Note that you can make the soufflés to the first-baked stage a few hours before the meal, then bake for the second time just before eating.

"These are fail-safe soufflés that anyone can make!"

Main Meals

Chicken & Lemongrass Skewers with Carrot & Cucumber Salad

PREPARATION TIME: 25 minutes, plus 15 minutes marinating time | COOKING TIME: 10 minutes | SERVES: 4

4 boneless, skinless
  chicken breasts, cut into
  bite-size pieces
1 tsp turmeric
2 tsp caster sugar
1 tsp soy sauce
1 red chilli, deseeded and
  finely chopped
1 small handful of micro
  coriander
1 tsp Thai red curry paste
8 lemongrass stalks, outer
  leaves removed and
  ends cut off
oil, for greasing
sea salt and freshly
  ground black pepper

CARROT & CUCUMBER
SALAD
2 carrots, peeled and cut
  into very thin slices
1/2 cucumber or
  2 Lebanese cucumbers,
  cut into very thin slices
2 spring onions, cut into
  fine 5cm/2in strips
1 red chilli, deseeded and
  finely diced
1 small handful of micro
  coriander
juice of 1 lime

TO SERVE
steamed basmati rice

South East Asian cuisine is a balance of three factors – sweet, sour and hot – so the first rule is to master that. When you get used to the basic ingredients of chilli, fish sauce, lime, coriander, ginger, garlic, lemongrass and kaffir limes, you can make amazingly aromatic dishes.

Put the chicken, turmeric, sugar, soy sauce, chilli, coriander and curry paste in a blender or food processor, season generously with salt and pepper and blitz to a smooth paste. Divide the paste into 8, then shape each portion around two-thirds of the lemongrass sticks, leaving a gap at one end as a handle. Cover with clear film and leave to one side.

To make the salad, toss together all the ingredients in a bowl until thoroughly combined. Season with salt and pepper, cover with clear film and put in the fridge for about 15 minutes for the flavours to develop.

When you are ready to eat, heat the grill to very high. Lay the chicken skewers on a lightly greased baking tray, then cook for 5 minutes on each side until cooked through and golden. Serve immediately with the rice and salad.

Roasted Chicken Breast with Hazelnut & Jerusalem Artichoke Couscous

PREPARATION TIME: 20 minutes | COOKING TIME: 20 minutes | SERVES: 4

200g/7oz Jerusalem
  artichokes, peeled and
  cut into small pieces
2 tbsp olive oil
4 boneless chicken
  breasts, skins on
150g/5½oz/heaped
  ¾ cup couscous
300ml/10½fl oz/scant
  1¼ cups chicken stock
50g/1¾oz butter
1 red onion, finely
  chopped
1 tsp finely chopped
  chives, plus extra to
  serve
2 heaped tbsp chopped
  flat-leaf parsley
50g/1¾oz/generous
  ⅓ cup hazelnuts,
  roughly chopped

DRESSING
5 tbsp olive oil
5 tsp hazelnut oil
2 tbsp cider vinegar
a pinch of caster sugar
sea salt and freshly
  ground black pepper

Couscous is really easy to prepare and is also a great vessel for different flavours. Whilst often paired with Middle Eastern or North African flavours, here it has an earthy nutty freshness to it, rounded off with the hazelnut oil dressing.

Preheat the oven to 200°C/400°F/Gas 6. Put the Jerusalem artichokes in a baking dish, drizzle with the oil and season with salt and pepper. Put in the oven and roast for 20 minutes until cooked and lightly browned.

Meanwhile, heat a frying pan over a medium-high heat. Season the chicken breasts on each side with salt and pepper, then put the breasts, skin-side down, in the pan. Cook for 7 minutes until golden, then transfer to a baking tray, skin-side up, and put in the oven with the artichokes. Roast in the oven for 10 minutes until cooked through. To test when they are ready, insert the tip of a sharp knife into the thickest part of the breasts – the juices should run clear.

While the artichokes and chicken are roasting, put the couscous in a large bowl. Bring the stock to the boil, then pour it over the couscous and fork through. Cover with clear film and leave to one side for 5 minutes, or until the stock is absorbed, then fork the couscous again.

Remove the chicken and artichokes from the oven. Set the chicken to one side. Add the butter, onion, chives, parsley, hazelnuts and roasted artichokes to the couscous and toss well.

In a small bowl or jug, whisk together all the dressing ingredients until thoroughly combined. Pour half the dressing into the couscous and mix until well combined. Season the couscous with salt and pepper.

Slice each of the chicken breasts against the grain on the diagonal and arrange on top of the couscous. Pour over the remaining dressing and serve sprinkled with chives.

Saffron-Poached Chicken with Parsley & Tarragon Gremolata

PREPARATION TIME: 25 minutes | COOKING TIME: 40 minutes | SERVES: 4

600ml/21fl oz/scant
  2½ cups chicken stock
150ml/5fl oz/scant
  ⅔ cups white wine
a large pinch of saffron
  threads
4 boneless, skinless
  chicken breasts
8 baby carrots, trimmed
4 heads of baby fennel,
  trimmed and cut in half
4 spring onions, trimmed
2 courgettes, cut into
  5mm/¼in-thick batons
sea salt and freshly
  ground black pepper

TARRAGON GREMOLATA
25g/1oz flat-leaf parsley,
  finely chopped
1 tsp grated orange zest
1 tsp grated lemon zest
1 small handful of
  tarragon
1 garlic clove, finely
  chopped
generous 3 tbsp olive oil

TO SERVE
boiled new potatoes
  (optional)

Saffron adds such a wonderful perfume and colour to dishes. Here I have gently poached some chicken and vegetables in a saffron infused stock then added extra layers of flavours with the Italian classic gremolata, changing the lemon to orange for extra aroma.

Pour the stock and wine into a saucepan and bring to the boil. Add the saffron threads, then reduce the heat to low and simmer for 5 minutes.

Meanwhile, to make the gremolata, put all the ingredients in a bowl and mix to combine. Season with salt and pepper and leave to one side.

Season the chicken with salt and pepper and bring the stock back to the boil. Put the chicken in the stock, reduce the heat to low again and simmer for 10 minutes. Remove the chicken from the stock, cover with foil and leave to one side to rest.

Meanwhile, put the carrots, fennel, spring onions and courgettes in the stock and cook for 5 minutes, then remove from the stock and keep warm. Increase the heat and simmer the stock for 15–20 minutes until it is reduced by half.

Cut each of the chicken breasts into slices against the grain on the diagonal. Put the chicken slices on top of the vegetables with a little stock spooned over. Add spoonfuls of the gremolata and serve immediately with boiled new potatoes, if you like.

Roasted Chicken Breasts Stuffed with Ricotta & Watercress

PREPARATION TIME: 10 minutes | **COOKING TIME: 35 minutes** | **SERVES: 4**

250g/9oz ricotta cheese
a large pinch of freshly
    grated nutmeg
50g/1¾oz watercress
400g/14oz new potatoes
150g/5½oz cherry
    tomatoes
2 red onions, quartered
2 garlic cloves
1 tbsp olive oil
4 boneless, skinless
    chicken breasts
sea salt and freshly
    ground pepper

TO SERVE
rocket
crusty bread

This is a really easy one-pan wonder of a dish. You can use all sorts of cheese to stuff the chicken: feta works well, as does garlicky goat's cheese. It's a rustic and colourful dish.

Preheat the oven to 200°C/400°F/Gas 6. Mix together the ricotta and nutmeg in a bowl and season with salt and pepper. Put a saucepan over a medium-low heat and wilt the watercress with a dash of water, then drain off any liquid and mix into the ricotta.

Put the potatoes, tomatoes, onions and garlic in a baking dish, drizzle with the oil and season with salt and pepper.

Put the chicken breasts on a chopping board and cut horizontally along the middle, keeping them "hinged" along one edge. Open out each breast to make a butterfly shape, then divide the ricotta mixture along the middle of the opened breast, across both halves. Roll up, securing the stuffed breast closed with one or two toothpicks. Put the chicken on top of the vegetables in the baking dish. Put in the oven and bake for 30 minutes, or until the chicken is cooked through. To test if the chicken is ready, insert the tip of a knife into the thickest part of one of the breasts – the juices should run clear.

Remove the chicken from the oven, slice each stuffed breast thickly on the diagonal and place on a plate with the vegetables. Serve with rocket and crusty bread.

Roast Chicken with Salsa Verde

PREPARATION TIME: 20 minutes, plus 20 minutes resting time | COOKING TIME: 1 hour 35 minutes | SERVES: 4

1.5kg/3lb 5oz chicken
1 lemon, halved
1 onion
olive oil, for drizzling
4 garlic cloves
500g/1lb 2oz butternut
  squash, halved,
  deseeded, peeled and
  cut into wedges
a pinch of chilli flakes
250g/9oz tenderstem
  broccoli
sea salt and freshly
  ground black pepper

SALSA VERDE
2 tinned anchovy fillets in
  oil, drained
1 garlic clove
juice and zest 1 lemon
1 tbsp baby capers,
  drained
1 large handful of herb
  mix, such as tarragon,
  parsley and mint,
  roughly chopped
100ml/3½fl oz/scant
  ½ cup olive oil

Roast chicken is always an easy fallback family dish, but sometimes I crave a variation. Here I have roasted it with butternut squash, served it with some green veggies and made a super-charged salsa verde dressing to accompany it.

Preheat the oven to 240°C/475°F/Gas 9. Wash the chicken inside and out under cold water and pat dry with kitchen paper. Season the chicken with salt and pepper, and stuff the cavity with the lemon halves and onion. Put the chicken in a roasting dish, drizzle with a little oil and put in the oven. After 15 minutes, turn the temperature down to 190°C/375°F/Gas 5 and roast the chicken for a further 1 hour 15 minutes or until cooked through. To test if the chicken is ready, insert the tip of a knife into the thickest part of the breast meat near the leg. The juices should run clear.

When 45 minutes into the roasting time, crush the garlic cloves with the flat edge of a knife, and put around the chicken with the butternut squash. Drizzle with a little oil, sprinkle over the chilli flakes and season with salt and pepper.

Meanwhile, make the salsa verde. Using a mortar and pestle or mini blender, crush the anchovies and garlic together. Tip into a bowl and add the lemon juice and zest, baby capers, herbs and oil. Stir until well combined. Season with salt and pepper and leave to one side.

When the chicken is cooked, remove from the oven, cover with foil, and leave to rest for 20 minutes. Shortly before it is time to eat, cook the broccoli in salted boiling water until al dente. Serve the roasted chicken with the broccoli and butternut squash, with the salsa verde drizzled over the top.

Chicken & Tamarind Stir-Fry with Mustard Seed Rice

PREPARATION TIME: 15 minutes | **COOKING TIME:** 40 minutes | **SERVES:** 4

1 tbsp vegetable oil
4 boneless, skinless chicken breasts, cut into bite-sized pieces
150g/5½oz sugar snap peas
1 red pepper, deseeded and cut into small pieces
4 spring onions, trimmed and cut into 2.5cm/1in pieces
2 garlic cloves, thinly sliced
1 small handful of purple basil leaves, roughly chopped
sea salt and freshly ground black pepper

MUSTARD SEED RICE
1 tsp vegetable oil
1 shallot, chopped
300g/10½oz/1½ cups basmati rice
2 tsp yellow mustard seeds
½ tsp turmeric

TAMARIND SAUCE
1 tsp tamarind syrup, or 2 tsp tamarind paste soaked in 2 tbsp water, then strained
½ tsp chilli powder
½ tsp cracked black pepper
1 tbsp soy sauce
1 tsp fish sauce
1 tsp caster sugar

Stir-fries are great quick supper dishes. You can throw in all sorts of vegetables and season to your own taste. I have used tamarind here for a touch of sourness, which you can buy in syrup or paste form in most supermarkets.

To make the mustard seed rice, heat the oil in a frying pan over a medium-low heat, add the shallot and fry gently for about 5 minutes until softened and translucent. Add the rice and mustard seeds, then pour over 600ml/21fl oz/ scant 2½ cups water. Add the turmeric, season with salt and pepper and stir to combine. Increase the heat to high and bring to the boil, then reduce the heat to low, cover and simmer for 20 minutes, or until the water has been absorbed and the rice is cooked through. Leave to one side, covered, while cooking the stir-fry.

Meanwhile, to make the tamarind sauce, mix together all the ingredients in a small bowl or jug until well combined.

Heat the oil in a wok or frying pan over a high heat, then, when the wok is very hot, add the chicken, season with salt and pepper and stir-fry for 5 minutes. Add the sugar snap peas, pepper and spring onions and cook for a further 5 minutes, then add the garlic and cook for 3 minutes more. Stir in the prepared tamarind sauce and the purple basil. When heated through, serve immediately with the Mustard Seed Rice.

Pan-Roasted Duck with Figs, Red Chard & Peppercorn Sauce

PREPARATION TIME: 15 minutes, plus 10 minutes resting time and making the mash (optional) |
COOKING TIME: 40 minutes | SERVES: 4

4 duck breasts
4 figs, quartered
2 tsp brown sugar
1 tsp pink peppercorns
100ml/3½fl oz/scant
 ½ cup Madeira
25g/1oz butter
100g/3½oz red chard,
 leaves and stalks
 separated, then
 chopped
sea salt and freshly
 ground black pepper

TO SERVE
Celeriac Mash (see page
 205) (optional)

Duck is an excellent meat. It has a bad press for being too fatty, but when cooked like this, slowly with the skin side down, it is beautiful. The figs are oozing with fragrant sweetness and the pink peppercorns (which are actually berries) add a delicate spiciness.

Preheat the oven to 180°C/350°F/Gas 4. Finely score the skin on the duck breasts with the tip of a sharp knife and season generously with salt and pepper. Heat an ovenproof frying pan over a low heat and lay the duck breasts, skin-side down, in the pan. Slowly cook the duck for 10–15 minutes, draining off the fat as you go, until the skin starts to turn crispy. Turn up the heat to brown the skin until crispy all over, then flip over the breasts and cook for a further 2 minutes. Transfer to the oven for 5 minutes, or until the duck breasts are firm to the touch but still quite pink inside. Remove from the oven, cover with foil and leave to rest for 10 minutes.

Meanwhile, drain any remaining fat from the pan, leaving behind the sediment. Put the pan over a medium heat, add the figs and brown sugar and cook for 3–4 minutes until caramelized. Add the peppercorns and cook for 1 minute, then add the Madeira and cook for a further 5 minutes until the sauce is reduced and thickened.

Melt the butter in a separate pan, add the red chard stems and cook for 2–3 minutes, then add the leaves and cook for 2 minutes or until wilted.

Slice the duck against the grain on the diagonal into slices and serve with the caramelized figs and red chard. Drizzle over the peppercorn sauce and serve with some celeriac mash, if you like.

Miso-Glazed Pork Belly with Stir-Fried Bok Choy

PREPARATION TIME: 25 minutes, plus overnight salting time | COOKING TIME: 2½ hours | SERVES: 4

150g/5½oz sea salt
150g/5½oz caster sugar
1.5kg/3lb 5oz piece pork
   belly

MISO GLAZE
100ml/3½fl oz/scant
   ½ cup mirin
50g/1¾oz/scant ¼ cup
   caster sugar
2 tbsp miso paste

BOK CHOY
1 tsp sesame oil
4 large bok choy,
   quartered, or 8 small
   bok choy, halved
1 red chilli, very finely
   chopped
1 tbsp soy sauce

TO SERVE
steamed rice

Pork belly is a fantastic cut: it's cheap and has great flavour. It works really well with Asian ingredients and in this dish I have cooked it in a miso glaze. The sweetness and saltiness really work together. The rice and bok choy keep the rest of the flavours clean and balanced.

Mix the salt and sugar in a jug with 500ml/17fl oz/2 cups warm water until dissolved. Put the pork belly in a deep bowl or baking dish and pour over the brine. Cover with clear film and put in the fridge to marinate overnight.

Preheat the oven to 180°C/350°F/Gas 4. Put the pork belly on a wire rack in a roasting dish, then pour in boiling water until it comes 2.5cm/1in up the sides of the dish. Cover the baking dish with foil and roast in the oven for 2 hours, or until the pork is very tender.

Meanwhile, make the miso glaze. Put the mirin and sugar in a saucepan over a medium heat and bring to the boil. Stir in the miso paste, remove the pan from the heat and then continue stirring until smooth. Leave to one side.

Remove the pork from the oven and increase the temperature to 200°C/400°F/Gas 6. Brush the pork with the miso glaze until well coated, then roast the pork, uncovered, for 30 minutes until the glaze is glistening and sticky.

Meanwhile, to make the bok choy, heat the sesame oil in a large frying pan, add the bok choy and stir-fry for about 5 minutes until starting to wilt. Add the chilli and the soy sauce and continue cooking for a further few minutes.

Remove the pork belly from the oven, slice it against the grain and place on the plate with the bok choy. Serve with rice.

"I love the wintery flavours of chestnut and quince with a touch of cinnamon: comfort food at its best."

Pork, Quince & Chestnut Casserole with Watercress Mash

PREPARATION TIME: 20 minutes | COOKING TIME: 1½ hours | SERVES: 4

2 tbsp olive oil
750g/1lb 10oz diced pork
100ml/3½fl oz/scant ½ cup white wine
2 onions, cut into wedges
2 quinces, peeled and sliced
250g/9oz tinned or vacuum-packed chestnuts
1 cinnamon stick
500ml/17fl oz/2 cups vegetable stock
1 sage sprig, leaves picked, plus extra to serve

WATERCRESS MASH
600g/1lb 5oz potatoes, peeled and cubed
1 tbsp olive oil
150g/5½oz watercress, roughly chopped
sea salt and freshly ground black pepper

Although we often think of Greek food as being very summery, with lots of salads and fish, in the winter it comes into its own in a different way. This casserole was inspired by winters in Greece, sitting by the log fire looking at views of the snow on the mountains.

Heat 1 tablespoon of the oil in a large frying pan over a high heat. Add the pork in batches, season with salt and pepper and sear until seared all over and browned. You want a good colour, as it adds flavour later. It will take about 15–20 minutes to sear all the pork. After the last batch is done, remove the pork from the pan and then pour in the wine and deglaze the pan for about 4 minutes, swishing the wine around and scraping the bits of pork off the base. Leave to one side.

In a separate saucepan, heat 1 tablespoon of the oil over a medium heat. Add the onion and quinces and cook, stirring occasionally, for 5 minutes, then add the chestnuts, cinnamon stick, pork and deglazed juices. Add the stock and sage leaves and bring to the boil. Reduce the heat to low and simmer for 1 hour, or until the pork is tender. Season with salt and pepper.

About 30 minutes into the cooking time, put the potatoes in a large saucepan, cover with water and bring to the boil. Turn the heat down to low and simmer, covered, for about 20 minutes until cooked through. Drain off the water, then add the remaining 1 tablespoon of oil and the watercress to the pan and mash with the potato. Season with salt and pepper, then serve with the casserole, sprinkled with sage leaves.

Smoked Tea- & Star Anise-Braised Pork Ribs with Pickled Cucumber

PREPARATION TIME: 15 minutes, plus 10 minutes pickling time | COOKING TIME: 2 hours | SERVES: 4

2l/70fl oz/8 cups vegetable stock
5cm/2in piece of root ginger, peeled and sliced
2 tbsp Russian caravan or lapsang souchong tea leaves
3 star anise
1kg/2lb 4oz pork ribs, cut into individual ribs

GLAZE
1 tsp Chinese five-spice
1 tbsp brown sugar
2 tbsp soy sauce
2 tbsp clear honey
1 tsp sesame oil

PICKLED CUCUMBER
70ml/2¼fl oz/scant ⅓ cup white wine vinegar
2 tsp caster sugar
1 tsp sea salt
1 cucumber, deseeded and thinly sliced crossways

TO SERVE
boiled rice (optional)

Cooking with tea is really interesting. The tea leaves in the stock give the ribs a smoky, earthy depth. The pickled cucumber is brilliant and goes with many dishes, including the Miso-Glazed Pork Belly (see page 92).

Pour the stock into a large saucepan and add the ginger, tea leaves and star anise. Bring to the boil, then reduce the heat to low and simmer for 5 minutes. Add the pork ribs and simmer, covered, for 1 hour, or until cooked through.

To make the pickled cucumber, put the vinegar and sugar in a saucepan and bring to the boil. Reduce the heat to low and simmer, stirring continuously, until the sugar has dissolved. Remove from the heat and leave to one side to cool completely. Meanwhile, mix together the salt and cucumber in a bowl and leave for 10 minutes, then tip the cucumber into a colander, rinse off the salt under cold water and drain well. Return the cucumber to the bowl, pour over the cooled vinegar mixture and toss well. Leave to one side.

To make the glaze, put all the ingredients in a small saucepan over a medium heat and bring to the boil. Reduce the heat to low and simmer for 5 minutes. Remove from the heat and leave to one side.

Preheat the oven to 200°C/400°F/Gas 6. When the ribs' braising time is up, remove them from the pan and drain in a colander. (You don't need the liquid for this recipe, but don't discard it, as it is a great stock for Asian soups.) Put the ribs on a baking tray and brush generously with the glaze. Put in the oven and cook for 45 minutes, occasionally brushing with extra glaze, until sticky and well cooked. Remove the ribs from the oven and serve with the pickled cucumber and boiled rice, if you like.

Pulled BBQ Pork with Red Cabbage Slaw

PREPARATION TIME: 25 minutes, plus 15 minutes resting time plus making the sauce and mayonnaise |
COOKING TIME: 3 hours | SERVES: 4

olive oil, for oiling and
  drizzling
2 tsp smoked paprika
1/2 tsp ground cumin
1/2 tsp ground coriander
1 tsp dried oregano
1 tsp turmeric
2 tsp garlic salt
1 tsp celery salt
1.5kg/3lb 5oz pork
  shoulder
100ml/3½fl oz/scant
  ½ cup BBQ Sauce
  (see page 198)
1 tbsp maple syrup
400g/14oz sweet
  potatoes, cut into
  wedges
sea salt and freshly
  ground black pepper

RED CABBAGE SLAW
1/2 small red cabbage,
  cored and finely sliced
2 carrots, peeled and
  grated
2 red apples, peeled,
  cored and grated
2 tbsp Mayonnaise
  (see page 199)
1 small red onion, finely
  chopped

TO SERVE
Deluxe Burger Buns
  (see page 201)
  (optional)

I have an almost obsessional craving for all-American dishes, such as BBQ pulled pork, ribs, etc. This is my BBQ pork recipe, which I have made a little fresher by serving it with a red cabbage and apple coleslaw instead of in a bun. Sweet potato wedges also go well with it.

Preheat the oven to 160°C/315°F/Gas 2–3 and oil a baking dish. Mix together all the spices, oregano, garlic salt and celery salt in a small bowl, then rub all over the pork joint. Put the pork in the oiled baking dish, cover the dish with foil and put on the middle shelf in the oven. Roast for 1 hour, undisturbed, then pour about 100ml/3½fl oz/scant ½ cup water into the dish. Cover again and leave to cook for a further 1½ hours.

Meanwhile, make the slaw. Toss together all the ingredients in a large bowl and season with salt and pepper. Cover with clear film and put in the fridge until needed.

After the pork has been in the oven for 2½ hours, whisk the bbq sauce and maple syrup together in a small bowl and brush over the pork. Put the pork back in the oven, uncovered, for a final 30 minutes. Meanwhile, put the sweet potato wedges on a baking tray, drizzle with oil and season with salt and pepper, then put in the oven on the shelf below the pork.

When the pork is cooked, remove from the oven, cover with foil and leave to rest for 15 minutes. Leave the sweet potato wedges in the oven until you are ready to serve.

Shred the pork meat into small pieces using two forks and pile up on a serving platter. Serve immediately with the red cabbage slaw and sweet potato wedges, and with the burger buns, if you like.

Rack of Lamb with Macadamia & Basil Crust

PREPARATION TIME: 25 minutes | COOKING TIME: 25 minutes | SERVES: 4

3 tbsp olive oil
2 lean racks of lamb,
  French trimmed and
  cut in half
12 asparagus spears
150g/5½oz mizuna,
  broken into the natural
  leaves
5 tsp balsamic vinegar

MACADAMIA & BASIL
CRUST
250g/9oz/1²/₃ cups
  macadamia nuts
2 tbsp chopped basil
  leaves
100g/3½oz/2 cups fresh
  breadcrumbs
150g/5½oz butter, cubed
sea salt and freshly
  ground black pepper

TO SERVE
crushed boiled new
  potatoes

Rack of lamb is a very impressive cut of meat to serve at a dinner. I've kept the rest of the dish very light, and the mizuna lettuce leaves mixed with lightly cooked asparagus make this a stunning meal. The lamb also goes well with new potatoes tossed in butter.

Preheat the oven to 200°C/400°F/Gas 6. To make the macadamia and basil crust, put all the ingredients in a blender or food processor and blitz until a fine paste forms. Season with salt and pepper and then briefly blitz again.

Heat 1 tablespoon of the oil in a heavy-based frying pan over a medium-high heat, then add the lamb racks and cook for about 8 minutes, turning occasionally, until golden brown and the meat is seared. You don't want to cook the lamb through at this stage.

Put the halved lamb racks in a roasting dish, fat-side facing up. Spread the macadamia and basil crust over the top of the meat, pressing it down firmly. Put in the oven and roast for 10 minutes – the meat should still be a little pink.

Meanwhile, bring a large saucepan of salted water to the boil. Drop in the asparagus and cook for 5 minutes, or until al dente. Put the mizuna in a bowl and dress with the remaining 2 tablespoons of oil and the balsamic vinegar. Add the asparagus spears and toss until well combined.

Remove the lamb from the oven and leave to rest for a few minutes. Cut each lamb rack into cutlets and serve with crushed boiled new potatoes and the mizuna and asparagus salad.

Lamb Skewers with Lentil Salad

PREPARATION TIME: 35 minutes, plus 8 hours marinating time or overnight, 10 minutes infusing and making the sauce and flatbreads | COOKING TIME: 15 minutes | SERVES: 4

½ onion, grated
2 garlic cloves, crushed
juice and zest of ½ lemon
a pinch of saffron threads
400g/14oz leg of lamb,
  bone removed and meat
  cut into chunks
5 tsp olive oil
sea salt and freshly
  ground black pepper

SALAD
6 radishes, finely sliced
½ cucumber or
  2 Lebanese cucumbers,
  finely sliced
4 spring onions, finely
  sliced
150g/5½oz drained,
  tinned lentils
1 handful of flat-leaf
  parsley leaves
1 handful of mint leaves
2 Little Gem lettuces,
  separated into leaves
½ tsp sumac
juice of 1 lemon
5 tsp olive oil

TO SERVE
Yogurt Sauce
  (see page 199)
4 plain Flatbreads
  (see page 202)

This dish was inspired by my travels in the Middle East. The marinade is inspired by Persian cooking methods and the salad has its roots in Lebanese cuisine. In fact, the salad is very similar to fattoush, with the tart, citrus-flavoured sumac.

Put the onion, garlic, lemon juice and zest and saffron in a large bowl and mix to combine. Leave to one side for 10 minutes to infuse, then add the lamb and oil, season with salt and pepper and toss until the lamb is well coated in the marinade. Cover with clear film and put in the fridge to marinate for 8 hours or overnight. Meanwhile, put 8 wooden skewers in cold water to soak.

When you are ready to cook the lamb, mix all the salad ingredients in a large bowl and toss until the leaves are well coated in the lemon juice and oil. Cover with clear film and put in the fridge while you cook the lamb.

Put a ridged griddle pan over a high heat. Thread the lamb cubes onto the soaked wooden skewers and season with salt and pepper. When the pan is very hot, chargrill the lamb skewers on all sides until the meat is cooked to your liking. It will take about 10–12 minutes in total for the lamb to be pink inside and golden brown on the outside. Serve the skewers with a pile of salad and some flatbreads and yogurt sauce on the side.

Sour Cherry Meatballs with Buttery Tagliatelle

PREPARATION TIME: 20 minutes | COOKING TIME: 45 minutes | SERVES: 4

250g/9oz veal mince
250g/9oz lamb mince
100g/3½oz/½ cup dried
  sour cherries or dried
  cranberries
50g/1¾oz /⅓ cup pine
  nut kernels, toasted
1 tsp ground allspice
½ tsp ground cinnamon
25g/1oz/½ cup fresh
  breadcrumbs
1 egg, beaten
1 tbsp olive oil
100g/3½oz butter
2 onions, roughly chopped
100ml/3½fl oz/scant
  ½ cup white wine
1 tbsp chopped flat-leaf
  parsley
250g/9oz tagliatelle
sea salt and freshly
  ground black pepper

These meatballs are a little different to the usual recipes. The pine nuts and sour cherries, with an added touch of spice, give them an exotic taste, and the buttery noodles soak up the flavours.

Put the veal and lamb, sour cherries, pine nuts, spices, breadcrumbs and egg in a large bowl. Season generously with salt and pepper and mix together until well combined, then shape the mixture into 16 small balls.

Heat the oil and half of the butter in a large frying pan over a medium heat. Add the onions and cook for 5 minutes, then reduce the heat to low and cook for a further 30 minutes, until softened and caramelized.

About 10 minutes before the end of the cooking time, heat a separate frying pan over a medium-high heat, add the meatballs and cook for 10 minutes until browned all over and cooked through. Tip the meatballs in with the onions, add the wine and cook for a further 10 minutes, then add the remaining butter and the parsley and stir through.

Meanwhile, put a large saucepan of water over a high heat, add a large pinch of salt and bring to a rapid boil. Add the tagliatelle and cook for 15 minutes, or according to the packet instructions. You want the pasta to be al dente. Drain the noodles into a colander, then add to the pan with the onions and meatballs. Season with salt and pepper, stir and serve.

"Meatballs have been done a million times, but these have another dimension of taste."

Chargrilled Rib Eye, Caramelized Shallots & Micro Watercress

PREPARATION TIME: 15 minutes | COOKING TIME: 30 minutes | SERVES: 4

1 tsp olive oil, plus extra
  for dressing
25g/1oz butter
400g/14oz shallots,
  topped and tailed
1 tsp caster sugar
generous 3 tbsp balsamic
  vinegar
4 rib eye steaks
200g/7oz micro
  watercress
sea salt and freshly
  ground black pepper

TO SERVE
shoestring chips or
  French fries (optional)

Classic flavour combos are there for a reason, and the best way to serve a steak is with some caramelized onions and a peppery watercress salad. Get your griddle pan as hot as possible and season the steak well.

Heat the oil and butter in a frying pan over a low heat. Add the shallots, cover the pan and cook very gently for about 20 minutes until golden brown, softened and caramelized. Stir in the sugar and balsamic vinegar and cook for a further 10 minutes, uncovered, until the liquid is reduced and sticky.

While the shallots are reducing, heat a ridged griddle pan over a high heat and season the steaks generously with salt and pepper. When the pan is hot, chargrill the steaks for about 4 minutes on each side for a medium-rare steak. Meanwhile, put the micro watercress in a bowl and dress with a splash of oil. Serve the steaks with the caramelized shallots spooned on top and the dressed micro watercress on the side, accompanied by shoestring chips, if you like.

My Ultimate Beef Burgers

PREPARATION TIME: 40 minutes, plus making the buns, mayonnaise and chutney | COOKING TIME: 15 minutes | SERVES: 4

2 tsp olive oil, plus extra
  for frying the burgers
1 large banana shallot,
  finely diced
400g/14oz rib eye steak
  or chuck beef, cut into
  chunks
1 egg
1 tsp Worcestershire
  sauce
1 tbsp ketchup
4 rashers of streaky
  bacon
8 slices of Cheddar cheese
½ crisp lettuce, shredded
8 Deluxe Burger Buns
  (see page 201), halved
Garlic Mayonnaise
  (see page 199)
4 large pickles, sliced
2 tomatoes, sliced
1 recipe quantity
  Quick Tomato Chutney
  (see page 200)
sea salt and freshly
  ground black pepper

So, claiming that my burgers are the ULTIMATE, ever, is quite a serious statement, but I stand by it. Customize at will, making them your personal, ultimate burgers. You can flavour the mayonnaise with wholegrain mustard or even truffle oil, or add blue cheese, Gruyère or even add fried onions to your burger. The options are endless, and the perfect burger is just waiting to be made...

Heat the oil in a frying pan over a medium heat, then add the shallot and cook for about 5 minutes until softened and translucent. Remove from the heat and leave to one side to cool.

Put the beef in a food processor and blitz until minced. Add the cooked shallots, egg, Worcestershire sauce and ketchup and season generously with salt and pepper. Blitz again to combine. Shape the beef mixture into 8 small burger patties, cover with clear film and put in the fridge.

Meanwhile, heat the grill to high and heat a frying pan over a high heat. Put the bacon on a grill rack and grill for about 5 minutes on each side until cooked and slightly crispy. Remove and cut in half. At the same time, add the remaining oil to the frying pan and then add the burger patties. Cook for 4–5 minutes on each side for juicy patties that are still pink inside, or increase the cooking time if you like them more well done. About 1–2 minutes before you think the patties will be ready, put a slice of cheese on top of each one.

Mix the lettuce with the garlic mayonnaise in a bowl, adjusting the amount used to taste, and divide between the burger bun bases. Put a couple of slices of pickle on the lettuce, followed by a slice of tomato, half a rasher of bacon and then a burger pattie. Spread a spoonful of the tomato chutney over the inside of the bun tops, then close the burgers and serve.

Marinated Hanger Steak with Sweet Potato Mash & Coriander-Honey Dressing

PREPARATION TIME: 25 minutes, plus 1 hour marinating time | COOKING TIME: 20 minutes | SERVES: 4

2 tbsp soy sauce
2 garlic cloves, finely chopped
1 tbsp olive oil
100ml/3½fl oz/scant ½ cup pineapple juice
2 x 500g/1lb 2oz hanger steaks
500g/1lb 2oz sweet potatoes, peeled and chopped

CORIANDER-HONEY DRESSING
1 red chilli, deseeded and roughly chopped
1 small handful of coriander
juice of 1 lemon
1 tsp clear honey
2 tbsp olive oil
sea salt and freshly ground black pepper

Hanger steak is a great cut that is full of flavour when served rare, so adjust the cooking time suggested according to the thickness of the steak. Here I have paired it with beta carotene-rich sweet potato and a light dressing similar to South America's chimichurri sauce.

Mix the soy sauce, garlic, oil and pineapple juice in a jug until well combined. Put the hanger steaks in a flat dish, then pour over the marinade. Roll the steaks in the marinade until well coated, then cover with clear film and put in the fridge to marinate for 1 hour.

Put the sweet potato in a saucepan, cover with lightly salted water and bring to the boil. Reduce the heat to low and simmer, covered, for 20 minutes or until cooked through. Drain off the water and mash with a little salt and pepper.

Meanwhile, heat a ridged griddle pan over a medium-high heat. Dry the steaks with kitchen paper then season generously with salt and pepper. Put the steaks in the hot pan and cook, turning often, for 8–10 minutes until browned but still quite pink in the middle.

Let the beef rest for 5 minutes before slicing it against the grain. While it is resting, make the dressing. Put all the ingredients in a blender and blitz until well combined but still with some texture. Drizzle the dressing over the steaks and serve with the sweet potato mash.

Beef Mole with Chilli & Coriander Cornbread

PREPARATION TIME: 25 minutes, plus making the cornbread | COOKING TIME: 1 hour–1 hour 10 minutes | SERVES: 4

4 tomatoes, quartered
2 onions, quartered
3 garlic cloves
2 tbsp olive oil
500g/1lb 2oz chuck or
    blade beef, cut into
    bite-size pieces
8–10 small shallots
2 dried chillies
1 tsp ground cinnamon
1 tsp ground coriander
300ml/10½fl oz/scant
    1¼ cups beef stock
1 tsp caster sugar
125g/4oz dark chocolate
1 tsp dried oregano
juice of 1 lime
sea salt and freshly
    ground black pepper

TO SERVE
1 large handful of
    coriander leaves,
    roughly chopped
1 recipe quantity warm
    Chilli & Coriander
    Cornbread (see
    page 180)
1 lime, quartered

This simple version of beef mole is quite mild, but it's a good introduction to Mexican cooking and I love the richness that the chocolate adds. The cornbread not only tastes divine but is also perfect for mopping up the juices and very quick to make.

Preheat the grill until very hot. Put the tomatoes, onions and garlic cloves on a baking tray and grill for 10 minutes until softened. Tip the vegetables into a blender or food processor and blitz until smooth.

While the vegetables are grilling, heat half of the oil in a frying pan over a high heat. Add the beef and cook, stirring occasionally, for 5–10 minutes until seared and browned. You want a good brown colour, as it adds flavour later in the dish.

Heat the remaining oil in a saucepan over a medium heat. Add the shallots and cook, stirring occasionally, for 10 minutes until browned. Add the beef to the saucepan, then add the dried chillies, cinnamon and coriander. Cook for 5 minutes, stirring occasionally, then add the blitzed tomato mix and stock. Cover and bring to the boil, then reduce the heat to low and simmer, stirring occasionally, for 30–40 minutes until the meat is tender. Season with salt and pepper, then add the sugar, chocolate, oregano and lime juice.

Serve sprinkled with the coriander, with some warm cornbread on the side and lime quarters to squeeze over.

Beef Rendang with Pineapple & Chilli Sambal

PREPARATION TIME: 30 minutes, plus making the curry paste and sambal | COOKING TIME: 1 hour | SERVES: 4

1 tbsp vegetable oil
750g/1lb 10oz rib eye
  steak or braising steak,
  cut into bite-size pieces
1 recipe quantity Curry
  Paste (see page 200)
200ml/7fl oz/generous
  ¾ cup beef stock
2 tbsp fish sauce
4 kaffir lime leaves,
  fresh or dried
1 cinnamon stick
4 lemongrass stalks,
  tough outer leaves
  removed and crushed
1 tbsp light brown
  muscovado sugar or
  palm sugar
1 small handful of micro
  coriander (or coriander
  leaves)
sea salt & freshly ground
  black pepper

COCONUT RICE
300g/10½oz/1½ cups
  Thai jasmine rice
100ml/3½fl oz/scant
  ½ cup coconut milk
1 tsp yellow mustard
  seeds

TO SERVE
Pineapple & Chilli Sambal
  (see page 199)

This is an excellent curry: thick, fragrant and rich. It's certainly a world away from your average take away! The pineapple sambal really adds balance, so do include it.

Heat the oil in a large frying pan over a medium-high heat. Add the rib eye and cook, stirring occasionally, for about 10 minutes until seared and browned. You want a good brown colour, as it adds flavour later. Transfer the beef to a saucepan, add the curry paste and cook for a further 5 minutes, then add the stock, fish sauce, kaffir lime leaves, cinnamon stick and lemongrass. Bring to the boil, then reduce the heat to low and simmer, stirring occasionally, for 40 minutes, until the sauce is thick and a rich golden brown and the meat is tender. If using braising steak, increase the simmering to 1 hour 10 minutes.

Meanwhile, make the coconut rice. Put the rice in a large saucepan with the coconut milk, mustard seeds and a pinch of salt. Add enough water to the pan so that the liquid comes to just under 1cm/½in above the rice. Cover the pan with a tight-fitting lid and bring to the boil, then reduce the heat to low and simmer for 20 minutes, or until the liquid has been absorbed and the rice is cooked. Remove from the heat, fluff up the rice with a fork, then cover again and let the steam separate the grains more. Leave to one side until required.

Add the sugar to the rendang and season with salt and pepper. Stir through the coriander, then serve with the coconut rice and Pineapple & Chilli Sambal on the side.

Beef, Bok Choy & Bamboo Shoot Stir-Fry

PREPARATION TIME: 20 minutes | COOKING TIME: 35 minutes | SERVES: 4

200g/7oz/1 cup white rice, such as Thai jasmine or basmati
600g/1lb 5oz rib eye steak, trimmed and cut into strips
2 tsp cornflour
generous 3 tbsp rice wine or sherry
1 tbsp soy sauce
2 tsp vegetable oil
1 tsp sesame oil
2.5cm/1in piece root ginger, peeled and finely chopped
2 garlic cloves, finely chopped
1 red chilli, deseeded and finely diced
1 red pepper, deseeded and sliced into strips
4 heads of bok choy, quartered
150g/5½oz drained, tinned bamboo shoots
sea salt and freshly ground black pepper

Stir-fries are so quick and easy. They are a great way to get veggies into your diet without being boring and they can be made very tasty with the addition of spices. This recipe can be adapted by using chicken, pork or prawns instead of the steak.

Tip the rice into a saucepan and add enough water so that the liquid comes to just under 1cm/½in above the rice. Cover with a tight-fitting lid and bring to the boil, then reduce the heat to low and simmer for 15–20 minutes until the water has been absorbed and the rice is cooked. Remove from the heat, fluff up the rice with a fork and then cover again and let the steam separate the grains more. Leave to one side until required.

Put the beef in a bowl and season with salt and pepper, then add the cornflour and toss until the beef is well coated. Mix the rice wine and soy sauce together in a small bowl.

With all the other stir-fry ingredients prepared and to hand, heat the vegetable oil in a wok or large frying pan until very hot. Stir-fry the beef in the oil for about 4 minutes until lightly cooked and brown, then turn out onto a plate.

Heat the wok or frying pan again until very hot, then add the sesame oil, ginger, garlic, chilli and all the vegetables. Stir-fry for 8 minutes, then add 1 tablespoon water and the rice wine mixture and toss through. Tip the beef and any juices back into the wok, and quickly toss until everything is combined and the beef has heated through. Serve immediately with the rice.

Venison Steaks with Pickled Red Cabbage & Truffle Polenta Fries

PREPARATION TIME: 20 minutes, plus 20 minutes setting time | COOKING TIME: 1 hour 30 minutes | SERVES: 4

vegetable oil, for frying
4 venison steaks
sea salt and freshly
  ground black pepper

PICKLED RED CABBAGE
1 tsp juniper berries
1 bay leaf
200ml/7fl oz/generous
  ¾ cup red wine vinegar
50g/1¾oz/heaped ¼ cup
  brown sugar
1 small red cabbage,
  cored and very finely
  sliced

TRUFFLE POLENTA FRIES
1l/35fl oz/4 cups
  vegetable stock
50g/1¾oz butter
200g/7oz/1⅓ cups
  instant polenta
125g/4½oz Parmesan
  cheese, grated
1 tbsp chopped truffle
  paste
1 tsp truffle oil
100ml/3½fl oz/scant
  ½ cup olive oil

Venison is not only very high in iron but also a very low-fat source of protein. The polenta chips make a great side dish, but are also satisfying if served by themselves as a nibble.

To make the truffle polenta fries, line a baking tin, about 18 x 25cm/7 x 10in, with clear film. Put the stock and butter in a saucepan and bring to the boil, then quickly pour in the polenta and stir well, removing any lumps. Reduce the heat to low and simmer, stirring continuously, for 15 minutes, then add 100g/3½oz of the Parmesan and season with salt and pepper. Add the truffle paste and oil and mix until well combined, then scrape the mixture into the lined tray. Leave to cool to room temperature, then put in the fridge for 20 minutes to set.

While the polenta is setting, make the pickled red cabbage. Put the juniper berries, bay leaf, vinegar and sugar in a saucepan and bring to the boil. Reduce the heat to low, add the red cabbage and stir well, then cover and simmer, stirring occasionally, for 40 minutes until the cabbage is cooked. Leave to one side.

When the cabbage is cooked, preheat the oven to 180°C/350°F/Gas 4. Turn the polenta out onto a chopping board and cut into 2cm/¾in wide x 8cm/3¼in long chips. Pour the olive oil into a large frying pan over a medium-high heat, and when hot, fry the polenta for 5 minutes until golden brown all over. Transfer the fries to a baking tray, sprinkle with the remaining Parmesan and put in the oven to keep hot.

Meanwhile, heat the vegetable oil in a separate frying pan over a medium-high heat. Season the venison with salt and pepper, then put in the hot pan and cook for about 6 minutes on each side, depending on thickness, until browned on the outside but still quite pink in the centre.

Serve the venison with the truffle polenta fries and warm pickled red cabbage.

112

"Venison is my favourite meat. It has a richness and texture that beef can lack."

Pan-Fried Sea Bass with Micro Herb & Pepper Salad

PREPARATION TIME: **25 minutes** | COOKING TIME: **10 minutes** | SERVES: **4**

2 carrots, peeled and cut into matchsticks
1 red pepper, deseeded and finely sliced
3 spring onions, finely sliced
4 sea bass fillets, skin on
1 tsp vegetable or groundnut oil
2 tbsp soy sauce
1 tsp mirin
1 tsp sesame oil
2.5cm/1in piece of root ginger, peeled and finely grated
1 small handful of micro cress
1 small handful of micro mizuna
1 small handful of micro coriander
1 small handful of micro Thai basil
sea salt and freshly ground black pepper

TO SERVE
300g/10½oz/1½ cups basmati rice (optional)

This is a simple dish, but people adore it. It is clean food and great for a detox menu or a daily dinner with some jasmine rice and steamed bok choy. This is what you want when you've been over-indulging in other parts of your life!

Put the carrots, pepper and spring onions in a serving bowl and toss together. Using a sharp knife, score the skin on the sea bass and season the fillets on both sides with salt and pepper.

Heat a large frying pan over a medium heat. Add the oil and then the sea bass fillets, skin-side down. Cook the fillets for about 8 minutes until the skin is crispy and golden and the fish is almost cooked through. Flip over the fillets and cook for 1 more minute – just enough to warm but not colour the flesh.

While the sea bass is cooking, mix the soy sauce, mirin, sesame oil and ginger together in a small bowl. Add the micro greens and herbs to the bowl of salad and dress with half the soy dressing.

Serve the sea bass with the salad and the remaining dressing drizzled over the top. Accompany with basmati rice, if serving.

Pan-Fried Salmon with Anchovy & Lemon Butter & Creamy Champ

PREPARATION TIME: **25 minutes** | COOKING TIME: **35 minutes** | SERVES: **4**

500g/1lb 2oz floury potatoes, such as Maris piper or King Edwards, cut into chunks
25g/1oz butter
5 tsp double cream
8 spring onions, finely sliced
2 tsp olive oil
4 salmon fillets, skin on
250g/9oz purple sprouting broccoli, trimmed
sea salt and freshly ground black pepper

ANCHOVY & LEMON BUTTER
2 anchovy fillets in oil, drained
zest of ¼ lemon
70g/2½oz unsalted butter, softened
¼ tsp lemon juice

The combination of healthy salmon with super-comforting champ is great. The sharp flavours in the anchovy and lemon butter add the perfect balancing touch.

To make the anchovy and lemon butter, blitz the anchovies and lemon zest in a mini blender until finely chopped. Add the butter and lemon juice, then blitz again to a smooth paste. Leave to one side.

Put the potatoes in a large saucepan, cover with water and bring to the boil. Reduce the heat to low and simmer, covered, for 20 minutes, or until cooked. Drain the potatoes into a colander and leave to steam dry for a few minutes, then return to the pan and mash with a potato masher or, for a finer texture, pass through a potato ricer or sieve. Add the butter, cream and spring onions and season generously with salt and pepper. Leave to one side and keep warm.

Bring a saucepan of water to the boil for cooking the sprouting broccoli and heat a frying pan over a medium heat. Pour the oil into the hot frying pan, then put the salmon fillets, skin-side down, in the pan. Cook for 8 minutes, or until golden and crispy, then flip over and cook for a further 4 minutes.

Meanwhile, add the broccoli to the boiling water and cook for 5 minutes until al dente. Drain well, then toss with the anchovy and lemon butter until well coated.

Serve the salmon with the champ and the sprouting broccoli. Drizzle any leftover melted butter over the top.

116

Mussels with Sauternes, Saffron & Micro Coriander

PREPARATION TIME: 15 minutes | COOKING TIME: 15 minutes | SERVES: 4

2kg/4lb 8oz mussels, scrubbed and de-bearded
1 tbsp olive oil
2 banana shallots, thinly sliced
4 garlic cloves, thinly sliced
a pinch of saffron threads
100ml/3½fl oz/scant ½ cup Sauternes or other dessert wine
generous 3 tbsp double cream
1 tbsp orange juice
1 large handful of micro coriander

TO SERVE
crusty bread

Sweet sauternes wine and saffron go very well together, and here I have combined them to make a wonderful rich broth in which to cook the mussels. Use ordinary coriander if no micro is available.

Scrub and clean the mussels in cold water, removing any grit, as many barnacles as you can and the beards. Rinse the mussels again under cold water for several minutes, and discard any muscles that have broken shells or that don't close as soon as they are tapped.

Heat the oil in a large saucepan over a medium-low heat, then add the shallots and garlic and fry, stirring occasionally, for 5 minutes until soft and translucent without any colour.

Turn the heat up to high and tip in the mussels, saffron and wine. Cover the saucepan with a tight-fitting lid and cook for 5 minutes. Remove from the heat, pour in the cream and orange juice and season with salt and pepper. Return the pan to the heat and cook, still covered, for a further 5 minutes. Discard any mussels that don't open.

Serve in deep bowls with the micro coriander sprinkled over the top and bread on the side.

Smoked Trout & Micro Coriander Coconut Rice

PREPARATION TIME: 20 minutes | COOKING TIME: 45 minutes | SERVES: 4

300g/10½oz/1½ cups
 Thai jasmine rice
100ml/3½fl oz/scant
 ½ cup coconut milk
1 tbsp vegetable oil
2 red chillies, deseeded
 and finely sliced
3 shallots, finely sliced
3 garlic cloves,
 finely chopped
2 spring onions,
 finely sliced
1 tbsp light soy sauce
2 eggs, beaten
1 small handful of
 micro coriander
 or coriander leaves
300g/10½oz smoked
 trout fillet, flaked

TO SERVE
150g/5½oz toasted
 coconut shavings
 (see page 154)
2 limes, cut into wedges

Coconut rice with smoked fish, herbs and specks of chilli is quite an unusual combination of flavours – a kind of Thai style kedgeree. In addition to being unusual, it tastes fantastic!

Tip the rice into a saucepan and cover with the coconut milk and enough water that the liquid comes to just under 1cm/½in above the rice. Cover with a tight-fitting lid and bring to the boil, then reduce the heat to low and simmer for 20 minutes, or until all the water has evaporated. Remove from the heat and fluff up the rice with a fork. Leave to one side, uncovered.

Heat the oil in a wok or frying pan over a medium heat. Add the chillies, shallots, garlic and spring onions and cook, stirring occasionally, for 8 minutes until fragrant and softened. Add the coconut rice and soy sauce, mix well and continue cooking for about 8 minutes until heated through. Make a little space to the side of the pan and add the beaten eggs. Whisk the eggs again lightly and cook for a further 2–3 minutes until the eggs are cooked.

Finally, add the coriander and smoked trout, toss all the ingredients until combined, including the cooked eggs, and cook for a further 5 minutes.

Serve with the toasted coconut shavings sprinkled over the top and with lime wedges on the side.

Pancetta-Wrapped Halibut with Clams & Celery Shoots

PREPARATION TIME: 10 minutes | COOKING TIME: 20 minutes | SERVES: 4

25g/1oz butter
4 carrots, peeled and
  thinly sliced on the
  diagonal
2 celery sticks, thinly
  sliced on the diagonal
150ml/5fl oz/scant
  2/3 cup stock
4 skinless halibut or
  cod fillets
8 thinly sliced strips
  of pancetta
1 tbsp olive oil
400g/14oz clams,
  washed under cold
  water
generous 3 tbsp
  white wine
100g/3½oz celery shoots

TO SERVE
crusty bread (optional)

Halibut is great when wrapped in cured pancetta. Here I have also braised some carrots and celery and added some lightly cooked clams. Serve this with crusty bread to soak up the flavours.

Heat the butter in a saucepan over a medium heat, then add the carrots and celery and stir until well coated in the butter. Add the stock and bring to the boil, then lower the heat and simmer, uncovered, for 20 minutes.

Meanwhile, cook the halibut and the clams. Wrap each halibut fillet in 2 strips of pancetta, keeping the seams on one side of the fish. Heat the oil in a large, deep frying pan over a medium heat, then put the halibut, seamless-side down, in the pan and cook for 4 minutes on each side or until golden brown on the outside and the flesh is milky coloured in the centre. Remove the fillets from the pan and cover with foil.

Turn the heat up and add the clams and wine. Cover the pan with a tight-fitting lid and cook for 5 minutes until the clams have opened, discarding any clams that are still closed.

Serve the halibut fillets with the carrot and celery mixture and the clams. Sprinkle with celery shoots and serve with crusty bread, if you like.

"Halibut is the king of fish with its wonderful close-textured flesh."

Soba Noodles with Crab & Micro Shiso Cress

PREPARATION TIME: **20 minutes** | COOKING TIME: **10 minutes** | SERVES: **4**

200g/7oz soba noodles
1 tsp sesame oil
1 tsp sesame seeds
1 tbsp soy sauce, plus extra for dressing the salad
a pinch of chilli powder
2 sheets nori seaweed, cut into strips with scissors
3 spring onions, finely sliced
100g/3½oz pickled pink ginger, finely chopped
1 tbsp bonito flakes (optional)
200g/7oz picked cooked white crab meat
1 small handful of micro shiso cress

Soba noodles are made with buckwheat flour, which is easier for people with wheat intolerences to digest. It is a classic Japanese dish, which is served cold with all the various condiments. I love this because it's super quick to make and very healthy.

Bring a large saucepan of water to a rapid boil, then drop in the soba noodles, separating them as you do so and stirring well to ensure they stay apart. Cook for 7–8 minutes or according to the packet instructions. Drain the noodles into a colander and wash under cold water until all the starch and gluten come out and the water runs clear. Tip into a bowl and toss with the sesame oil to stop the noodles sticking together.

Mix the sesame seeds, soy sauce and chilli powder together in a small bowl, then add to the noodles and toss until well combined. Cover with clear film and put in the fridge while you prepare the rest of the accompaniments.

Serve the noodles on a large plate with the crab meat on top. Put the seaweed, spring onions, pickled ginger and bonito flakes, if using, around the edge. Finally, mix the micro mizuna and micro shiso cress together, dress in a little soy sauce and scatter over. Serve immediately.

Crab & Saffron Risotto

PREPARATION TIME: 20 minutes | COOKING TIME: 40 minutes | SERVES: 4

800ml/28fl oz/scant
   3½ cups fish stock
1 tbsp olive oil
1 onion, finely diced
2 garlic cloves, finely
   chopped
200g/7oz/heaped 1 cup
   risotto rice, such as
   Arborio
100ml/3½fl oz/scant
   ½ cup white wine
a large pinch of saffron
   threads
8 spring onions, finely
   sliced
400g/14oz picked cooked
   white crab meat
50g/1¾oz butter
1 tbsp chopped flat-leaf
   parsley
zest of 1 lemon, to taste

Many people seem to think that risottos are hard to make, but they just need a little love and attention. Keep stirring them to release the starch in the grains and don't overcook the rice. When you master the art of risottos, you can then experiment with all sorts of flavours.

Put the stock in a saucepan and bring to the boil. Heat the oil in a deep frying pan over a medium heat, then add the onion and garlic and cook for 5 minutes until softened and translucent. Add the rice and stir to coat with the oil.

Pour in the wine and stir until it is all absorbed, then add a ladleful of the hot stock and stir until it is fully absorbed by the rice. Add the saffron, then continue to add the stock, ladleful by ladleful, stirring the rice after each addition until all the stock is absorbed. After 20 minutes, add the spring onions and cook for a further 5 minutes, stirring continuously, then add the crab meat and butter and stir until smooth and creamy. Check the rice: you want it to be cooked but still with a little bite. Add more stock if it needs further cooking.

When the rice is ready, add the parsley and the lemon zest, to taste. Remove the pan from the heat and leave the risotto to sit for 5 minutes before serving.

Prawn, Pea Shoot & Lemon Linguine

PREPARATION TIME: 15 minutes | COOKING TIME: 25 minutes | SERVES: 4

400g/14oz linguine
2 tbsp olive oil, plus extra
  for drizzling
400g/14oz peeled raw
  king prawns, deveined
1 red chilli, deseeded and
  finely chopped
juice and zest of 1 lemon
25g/1oz pea shoots
1 small handful of flat-
  leaf parsley leaves,
  chopped
sea salt and freshly
  ground black pepper

This light, fresh pasta dish is perfect for lunch. You can replace the prawns with white crab meat or have a vegetarian version with just peas and the pea shoots. Adding the pasta along with a little cooking liquid to the prawns, then cooking a bit more, is the true Italian way.

Bring a large saucepan of lightly salted water to the boil. When boiling rapidly, add the linguine and cook for 20 minutes, or according to the packet instructions, until al dente.

About halfway through the pasta cooking time, heat the oil in a frying pan over a medium heat. Add the prawns and stir-fry for 4 minutes, then add the chilli and cook for a further 4 minutes, or until the prawns have turned pink and are cooked through.

Drain the pasta, leaving a tablespoon of cooking water, and add to the pan with the prawns, along with the lemon juice and zest, pea shoots and parsley. Stir-fry over the heat for 1–2 minutes until all the ingredients are well mixed and the pasta is heated through. Finally, add a good drizzle of olive oil and season with salt and pepper. Serve immediately.

Chargrilled Tuna with Caponata & Basil

PREPARATION TIME: 20 minutes, plus making the mash | COOKING TIME: 1 hour | SERVES: 4

50g/1¾oz pine nut kernels

2 tbsp olive oil, plus extra for frying

1 onion, chopped

3 garlic cloves, finely chopped

2 celery sticks, cut into 1cm/½in cubes

1 red pepper, deseeded and cut into 1cm/½in cubes

2 courgettes, cut into 1cm/½in cubes

1 aubergine, cut into 1cm/½in cubes

400g/14oz canned chopped tomatoes

5 tsp balsamic vinegar

4 tbsp caster sugar

4 tuna steaks each weighing 180–200g/6–7oz

1 large handful of basil

sea salt and freshly ground black pepper

TO SERVE
Roasted Garlic & Olive Oil Mash (see page 204)

Caponata is a southern Italian slightly sweet and sour vegetable stew, not dissimilar to ratatouille. It's also great served cold with cured meats and cheese.

Heat a frying pan over a medium-high heat, then add the pine nuts and dry-roast until fragrant and starting to brown. Leave to one side.

Heat 1 tablespoon of the oil in a large saucepan over a medium heat, then add the onion, garlic and celery and fry for 10 minutes until softened and translucent, stirring occasionally. Season with salt and pepper, then add the pepper and courgettes and continue cooking.

Meanwhile, heat the remaining tablespoon of oil in the frying pan over a very high heat. Add the aubergine in batches and fry each batch, stirring occasionally, for about 5 minutes until slightly coloured.

Add the aubergine and tomatoes to the onion mixture and bring to the boil, then reduce the heat to low and simmer for 30–40 minutes until thick and rich. Add the balsamic vinegar and sugar, check the seasoning, and then add the toasted pine nuts.

Heat a ridged griddle pan over a high heat until smoking hot. Lightly oil both sides of the tuna steaks and season with salt and pepper. Add the tuna to the griddle pan and chargrill for 3–4 minutes on each side until seared but still pink in the middle. Adjust the cooking time according to the thickness of the steaks and personal preference.

Serve the tuna steaks with the Roasted Garlic & Olive Oil Mash and the caponata spooned over the top, sprinkled with the micro basil.

Pad Thai

PREPARATION TIME: 20 minutes | COOKING TIME: 15 minutes | SERVES: 4

250g/9oz rice noodles
2 tbsp dried shrimps
1 tbsp groundnut oil,
    plus extra for dressing
2 shallots, sliced
3 garlic cloves, finely
    chopped
150g/5½oz raw peeled
    and deveined king
    prawns
100g/3½oz fried tofu,
    cut into cubes or strips
2 eggs, beaten
150g/5½oz bean sprouts
4 spring onions or
    Chinese chives,
    roughly sliced
1 small handful of
    coriander leaves

PAD THAI SAUCE
1 tsp chilli powder
1 tbsp fish sauce
1 tbsp light soy sauce
1 tbsp tamarind water
1 tbsp caster sugar

TO SERVE
50g/1¾oz peanuts,
    finely chopped
2 limes, cut into wedges

This is a classic dish that gets completely destroyed by takeaways and pubs all over the world. It is quite sophisticated, and does need some delicate balancing. Practise your Pad Thai sauce and personalize it to your tastes, adding more chilli for heat, more tamarind for sour and more sugar for sweetness. A brilliant dish.

To make the sauce, whisk all the ingredients together in a small bowl until well combined and leave to one side.

Put the rice noodles in a heatproof bowl, cover with boiling water and leave to soak for 10 minutes. Drain the noodles into a colander and wash under cold water. Return the noodles to the bowl and dress in a little oil to prevent them from sticking together. Meanwhile, put the dried shrimps in a separate bowl, cover with hot water and soak for 5 minutes, then drain.

Heat the oil in a wok or large frying pan over a medium heat. Add the shallots, garlic, soaked shrimps and king prawns and stir-fry for 5 minutes. Add the tofu, soaked noodles and Pad Thai sauce and cook for a further 8 minutes, stirring occasionally. Make a little space to the side of the pan and add the beaten eggs. Whisk the eggs again lightly and cook for a further 2–3 minutes until the eggs are cooked. Finally, add the bean sprouts, spring onions and coriander and toss all the ingredients together, including the cooked eggs, until combined.

Serve sprinkled with the chopped peanuts and with lime wedges on the side.

Chargrilled Prawns with Mango

PREPARATION TIME: 15 minutes | COOKING TIME: 8 minutes | SERVES: 4

1 red chilli, deseeded and finely chopped
2 garlic cloves, minced
1 tbsp olive oil
2 ripe mangoes
500g/1lb 2oz raw peeled and deveined king prawns
1 head of Little Gem lettuce, leaves separated
sea salt and freshly ground black pepper

TO SERVE
juice of 1 lime
1 small handful of micro coriander

This is a really simple salad and is very delicious, despite its simplicity. The flavours are clean and vibrant. If I can find good quality crab meat or even lobster, I use that too.

Whisk together the chilli, garlic and olive oil in a large bowl, then add the prawns and toss well.

Using a sharp knife, carefully slice each mango down both sides, avoiding the stone. Peel the skin off the mango sides, then cut the flesh into slices. Peel the remaining parts of the mango and slice the flesh from the stone. Leave the flesh to one side.

Heat a ridged griddle pan over a very hot heat, then add the prawns, season with salt and pepper and cook for 4 minutes on each side or until the prawns have turned pink and are cooked through.

To serve, arrange the mango slices on the lettuce, then top with the prawns. Squeeze over the lime juice and sprinkle over the micro coriander.

Summer Vegetable & Truffle Oil Pizzas

PREPARATION TIME: 20 minutes, plus making the pizza dough | COOKING TIME: 45 minutes | SERVES: 4

4 courgettes
2 tsp olive oil
250g/9oz drained, tinned artichoke hearts, halved
200g/7oz bottled roasted red peppers, cut into strips
1 recipe quantity Pizza Dough, formed into 4 pizza bases (see page 204)
truffle oil, to drizzle
150g/5½oz Parmesan cheese, grated
100g/3½oz micro basil, micro mizuna or a combination of both

CARAMELIZED SHALLOT PURÉE
50g/1¾oz butter
8 banana shallots, sliced
1 thyme sprig, leaves picked
1 tsp caster sugar
4 tsp double cream
sea salt and freshly ground black pepper

This variation on a pizza was inspired by a trip to the south of France. I have kept the traditional thin crust, but then made a caramelized shallot purée instead of a tomato base. It's topped with summery veggies, Parmesan cheese and a drizzle of truffle oil to create a deluxe, seriously morish pizza.

To make the caramelized shallot purée, melt the butter in a frying pan over a medium-low heat, then add the banana shallots and thyme and fry gently for 20 minutes until the shallots are softened and translucent. Add the sugar and cream, cover and cook for a further 15 minutes until caramelized, then season with salt and pepper. Put the mixture in a food processor or blender and blitz to a fine purée. If the mixture looks too thin for a good pizza base topping, return it to the pan and cook very gently, stirring occasionally, until the excess liquid has evaporated.

Preheat the oven to 200°C/400°F/Gas 6 and put two baking sheets in the oven to heat up.

Slice the courgettes lengthways into thin ribbons using a swivel-bladed vegetable peeler, then put in a bowl with the olive oil, artichoke hearts and peppers and toss until well combined.

Fork the pizza bases all over and put on the hot baking sheets. Spread the caramelized shallot purée evenly over the bases, then arrange the dressed vegetables on top. Put the pizzas in the oven and bake for 8–10 minutes until cooked and golden, then remove from the oven, drizzle with some truffle oil and sprinkle over the Parmesan and micro herbs. Serve immediately.

"Spelt's nutty, earthy undertones and chewy texture work very well in risottos."

Spelt & Roast Butternut Squash Risotto

PREPARATION TIME: 15 minutes | COOKING TIME: 1 hour | SERVES: 4

350g/12oz butternut
squash, halved,
deseeded, peeled
and diced
2 tbsp olive oil
1 litre/35fl oz/4 cups
vegetable stock
1 onion, finely diced
2 garlic cloves, finely
chopped
200g/7oz spelt grains
100ml/3½fl oz/scant
½ cup white wine
1 tbsp chopped fresh sage
25g/1oz butter
50g/1¾oz Parmesan
cheese, grated
sea salt and freshly
ground black pepper

TO SERVE
25g/1oz rocket leaves
25g/1oz pumpkin seeds
balsamic vinegar

I have used butternut squash and sage for the flavourings in this hearty risotto, but wild mushrooms, chicken, asparagus and Jerusalem artichokes would all work well too.

Preheat the oven to 200°C/400°F/Gas 6. Put the butternut squash on a baking tray, drizzle with 1 tablespoon of the oil and season with salt and pepper. Bake in the oven for 15 minutes until cooked.

Meanwhile, put the stock in a saucepan and bring to the boil, then reduce to a simmer. At the same time, heat the remaining tablespoon of oil in a deep frying pan over a medium heat, then add the onion and garlic and cook for 5 minutes until softened and translucent. Add the spelt grains and stir to coat with the oil.

Pour in the wine and stir until it is all absorbed, then add a ladleful of the hot stock and stir until it is fully absorbed by the spelt. Continue to add the stock, ladleful by ladleful, stirring the spelt to absorb the stock after each addition. This will take 30–40 minutes in total. About 20 minutes into the spelt cooking time, add the butternut squash and sage.

During the latter part of the cooking process, check the spelt regularly. You want it to be cooked but still with a little bite, and you may not need all the stock. When it is just about the desired consistency, add the butter and Parmesan and season with salt and pepper.

Serve the risotto with the rocket leaves and pumpkin seeds sprinkled over the top and a good drizzle of balsamic vinegar.

Herb & Ricotta Ravioli
with Buttered Rainbow Chard

PREPARATION TIME: 20 minutes, plus 30 minutes resting time and making the dough | COOKING TIME: 10 minutes | SERVES: 4

400g/14oz ricotta cheese
1 small handful of basil
1 small handful of mint
a pinch of freshly grated nutmeg
1 recipe quantity Pasta Dough (see page 203), rolled into 2 sheets
1 egg yolk, beaten
semolina, for dusting
50g/1¾oz butter
50g/1¾oz yellow and red rainbow chard, leaves and stalks separated
sea salt and freshly ground black pepper

TO SERVE
grated Parmesan cheese

Making your own pasta is a great habit to form. It is much easier than you'd think and the results are very satisfying. These are delicate herb raviolis with chard, but you can make many variations. My other fave is squash and amaretti with sage brown butter.

Put the ricotta, herbs and nutmeg in a blender or food processor and blitz until smooth. Tip the ricotta mixture into a bowl, season with salt and pepper, then cover with clear film and put in the fridge for 30 minutes or until needed.

Lay one pasta dough sheet on a large chopping board. Put individual heaped teaspoonfuls of the ricotta filling all over the sheet at 3cm/1¼in intervals. Brush around the filling with the beaten egg yolk, then put the second sheet of pasta over the top. Carefully press down around the filling mounds to seal the sheets together, then, using a sharp knife or a ravioli cutter, cut into squares. Put the ravioli on a tray dusted with semolina.

Bring a large saucepan of lightly salted water to the boil. When boiling rapidly, add the ravioli and cook for 8 minutes until al dente.

Meanwhile, melt the butter in a large frying pan over a medium-low heat. Add the rainbow chard stalks and cook for 2–3 minutes, then add the leaves and cook for 2 minutes until wilted.

When the pasta is cooked, drain in a colander and then gently toss together with the chard in the pan. Season with salt and pepper and serve immediately with plenty of grated Parmesan on top.

"Gnocchi should be light little pillows that melt in the mouth."

Potato Gnocchi with Pea Shoot Pesto & Pecorino Shavings

PREPARATION TIME: 15 minutes | COOKING TIME: 1 hour 15 minutes | SERVES: 4

1kg/2lb 4oz floury
  potatoes, such as King
  Edwards, scrubbed
1 egg, beaten
300g/10½oz plain flour
50g/1¾oz butter
sea salt and freshly
  ground black pepper

PEA SHOOT PESTO
150g/5½oz Pecorino
  cheese
150g/5½oz pea shoots
1 small handful of basil
2 garlic cloves
50g/1¾oz pine nut
  kernels
150ml/5fl oz/scant ⅔ cup
  olive oil

I started making gnocchi when I was in Sardinia, where I fell in love with the region's Pecorino Sardo, which is a smooth, slightly salty hard cheese that is fantastic in pesto. Gnocchi should have a light texture, so do not add too much flour, as this will make them heavy.

Preheat the oven to 200°C/400°F/Gas 6. Put the potatoes on a baking tray and bake in the oven for 1 hour, or until cooked through.

Meanwhile, make the pesto. Set aside 50g/1¾oz of the pecorino cheese and put all the remaining ingredients in a blender or food processor and blitz to a rough paste. Season with salt and pepper and leave to one side. Using a swivel-bladed vegetable peeler, slice the remaining Pecorino into shavings. Leave to one side.

Remove the potatoes from the oven, cut them in half and scoop the flesh into a bowl. Keeping the potato covered with a tea towel so it doesn't dry out and go hard, gradually pass it through a coarse sieve, potato ricer or a mouli into a large bowl. Add the egg and flour to the sieved potato and mix into a soft dough. Be careful not to overwork the dough, as it will go gluey and tough.

Bring a large saucepan of lightly salted water to a rapid boil. Roll the dough on a lightly floured surface into sausage shapes roughly 2.5cm/1in wide and 38cm/15in long, then cut into 2.5cm/1in pieces and lay on a floured plate. Add half the gnocchi to the saucepan of boiling water, cook for 5 minutes and then drain. Repeat with the remaining gnocchi.

Melt the butter in a frying pan over a medium heat. Add the gnocchi to the pan, season with salt and pepper and fry for 5 minutes, turning over occasionally, until lightly coloured. Add the pesto and mix until the gnocchi is well coated. Serve immediately, sprinkled with the Pecorino shavings.

Broccoli & Sweet Potato Tempura

PREPARATION TIME: 20 minutes, plus making the sauce and noodles | COOKING TIME: 35 minutes | SERVES: 4

500ml/17fl oz/2 cups
    vegetable oil
200g/7oz tenderstem
    broccoli, trimmed
2 sweet potatoes, thinly
    sliced

RADISH & CARROT SALAD
50g/1¾oz white radish,
    cut into matchsticks
50g/1¾oz carrot, cut into
    matchsticks
1 tsp sesame seeds
1 tbsp soy sauce

TEMPURA BATTER
50g/1¾oz/heaped ⅓ cup
    cornflour
200g/7oz/2⅔ cups plain
    flour
300ml/10½fl oz/scant
    1¼ cups sparkling
    water, very cold
sea salt and freshly
    ground black pepper

TO SERVE
Dipping Sauce (see page
    198)
Crab & Micro Shiso
    Cress (see page 123)
    (optional)

The secret to my tempura is to use cornflour and sparkling water for extra bubbles of air, making a super-light batter. I have used broccoli and sweet potato for contrasting colours. This batter and sauce also go well with king prawns, white fish and calamari.

To make the salad, toss together the radish, carrot, sesame seeds and soy sauce in a small bowl until well combined, then leave to one side.

Preheat the oven to 140°C/275°F/Gas 1 and put a baking sheet in to heat up.

Heat the oil in a large, heavy-based saucepan over a medium heat until hot, being very careful not to overheat the oil. It will be hot enough when a piece of vegetable dropped into the oil sizzles. When the oil is hot, make the tempura batter by whisking the cornflour, flour and water together in a large bowl until smooth, seasoning with salt and pepper. (You make this at the last minute so that the bubbles stay in the batter.)

One piece at a time, dip the broccoli and sweet potato pieces in the batter, then carefully drop into the hot oil and deep-fry for 6–8 minutes until a light golden brown. Don't put too many pieces in the oil at the same time, as the temperature of the oil will drop. Scoop the tempura out, using a slotted spoon, and drain on kitchen paper. Transfer to the heated baking tray to keep warm. Cook the remainder in batches, adding them to the oven, until all the pieces of broccoli and sweet potato have been cooked.

Serve the tempura with the radish and carrot salad and the dipping sauce on the side, and with the Crab & Micro Shiso Cress, if you like.

Desserts

White Chocolate & Ginger Cream with Passion Fruit Curd

PREPARATION TIME: 15 minutes, plus 15 minutes cooling time and 2 hours setting time | COOKING TIME: 10 minutes | SERVES: 4

300ml/10½fl oz/scant 1¼ cups double cream
500g/1lb 2oz white chocolate, finely chopped, plus shavings to decorate
2 tsp chopped preserved stem ginger

PASSION FRUIT CURD
8 passion fruit
100g/3½oz/heaped ⅓ cup caster sugar
2 eggs, plus 2 egg yolks
25g/1oz unsalted butter

White chocolate and ginger are great together, and make an unusual dessert when topped with this passionfruit curd. The curd will keep in the fridge for about a week and is amazing served on pancakes, toast and crumpets.

To make the passion fruit curd, halve the passion fruit and scoop the flesh and seeds into a saucepan. Add the sugar, eggs and egg yolks and whisk until well combined, then put the saucepan over a medium heat and stir slowly for a few minutes until the egg mixture thickens.

Add the butter and stir quickly until it melts and the ingredients are well combined. Remove from the heat and leave to cool to room temperature, then cover with clear film and put in the fridge to chill for 1 hour.

Meanwhile, to make the white chocolate and ginger cream, heat the cream in a small saucepan over a medium heat until it just begins to boil. Remove from the heat and stir in the chocolate. When melted and well combined, stir in the ginger.

Divide the chocolate mixture among four glass serving dishes, leaving a minimum gap of 1cm/½in at the top. Put in the fridge to set for at least 2 hours, then top with the passion fruit curd in an even layer and decorate with white chocolate shavings.

Chocolate Fondants with Mint Ice Cream

PREPARATION TIME: 20 minutes, plus 30 minutes infusing time, 30 minutes chilling time, 40 minutes churning time and 1 hour freezing time | COOKING TIME: 15 minutes | SERVES: 4

150g/5¹/₂oz dark chocolate, 70% cocoa solids
150g/5¹/₂oz unsalted butter, plus extra for greasing
3 eggs, plus 3 egg yolks
150g/5¹/₂oz/heaped ²/₃ cup caster sugar
1 tsp salt
125g/4¹/₂oz/1 cup plain flour
2 tbsp unsweetened cocoa powder, plus extra for dusting

MINT ICE CREAM
500ml/17fl oz/2 cups double cream
250ml/9fl oz/1 cup whole milk
3 handfuls of mint leaves
5 egg yolks
150g/5¹/₂oz/heaped ²/₃ cup caster sugar

To make the ice cream, pour the cream and milk into a saucepan and bring to the boil slowly, stirring continuously. Add two of the handfuls of mint, reduce the heat to low and simmer for 5 minutes, then remove from the heat and leave to infuse for 30 minutes. Strain the infused mixture through a fine sieve into a clean saucepan.

Whisk together the egg yolks and sugar in a large bowl until well combined but not so light that there are bubbles in the mixture. Bring the infused mint cream to the boil over a medium heat, then pour it into the egg mixture, whisking continuously so that the eggs do not cook. Pour the custard mixture back into the saucepan and heat very gently, stirring continuously, until thickened. Remove from the heat, pour into a bowl and leave to cool slightly, then put in the fridge for 30 minutes to chill completely. Once chilled, stir in the remaining mint and pour the custard into an ice-cream machine. Churn according to the manufacturer's instructions, then transfer to a plastic or metal container, cover and freeze. Alternatively, if you do not have an ice-ceam machine, refer to the instructions for freezing on page 161.

To make the fondants, preheat the oven to 180°C/350°F/Gas 4. Grease four 125ml/4fl oz/¹/₂ cup pudding basins or ramekins and dust with cocoa powder. Put the chocolate and butter in a heatproof bowl and rest it over a saucepan of gently simmering water, making sure the bowl does not touch the water. Heat, stirring occasionally, until the chocolate and butter have melted.

Put the eggs, egg yolks, sugar and salt in a bowl, then whisk until pale and slightly thickened. Meanwhile, sift the flour and cocoa powder together. Fold the chocolate mixture into the creamed eggs and sugar, then fold in the sifted flour and cocoa. Spoon the mixture into the prepared pudding basins and put in the oven. Bake for 8 minutes until just set. Meanwhile, remove the ice cream from the freezer to soften slightly. Remove the chocolate fondants from the oven and serve immediately with a large scoop of mint ice cream on top.

Cinnamon Lebanese Pudding with Almonds & Pistachios

PREPARATION TIME: 15 minutes, plus 24 hours soaking time and 2 hours chilling time | COOKING TIME: 50 minutes | SERVES: 4

70g/2½oz/½ cup unblanched almonds
70g/2½oz/½ cup shelled pistachio nuts
250ml/9fl oz/1 cup mineral water
125g/4½oz/scant ¾ cup ground rice
100g/3½oz/heaped ⅓ cup caster sugar
½ tbsp ground caraway
2½ tsp cinnamon
1¼ tsp ground aniseed
½ tbsp desiccated coconut
edible gold leaf (optional)

This dessert is called *meghli* in Lebanon, where it is served when a baby is born. It is a rich, highly spiced ground rice pudding and I have topped it with soaked almonds, pistachios and gold leaf. When you soak nuts, they sprout and become nutrient-dense.

Put the almonds and pistachios in a large bowl and pour over the mineral water. Leave for 24 hours at room temperature, then drain and rinse. Put the soaked nuts in an airtight container and leave in the fridge.

Pour 1.4l/48fl oz/5½ cups water into a large saucepan and bring to the boil. Add the ground rice, sugar and spices and stir well, then bring back to the boil. Simmer, uncovered, stirring occasionally, for 45 minutes until the mixture is very thick.

Spoon the rice mixture into four 150ml/5fl oz/scant ⅔ cup glass bowls or pretty pots. Cover with clear film, pressing it onto the surface so that a skin doesn't form, then put in the fridge to chill for 2 hours.

Top the desserts with a mixture of soaked almonds and pistachios, then sprinkle over the desiccated coconut and decorate with pieces of gold leaf, if you like. Any leftover nuts can be put back in the fridge for snacking on.

Greek Rhubarb & Custard Filo Pie

PREPARATION TIME: 25 minutes | **COOKING TIME:** 1 hour 10 minutes | **SERVES:** 12

8 sticks of rhubarb,
  trimmed
100g/3½oz/heaped
  ⅓ cup caster sugar
100g/3½oz butter,
  melted, plus extra for
  greasing
10 sheets of filo pastry

CUSTARD FILLING
350ml/12fl oz/scant
  1½ cups milk
2 tsp vanilla extract
50g/1¾oz/heaped ⅓ cup
  fine semolina
100g/3½oz/heaped
  ⅓ cup caster sugar
2 eggs, beaten

SYRUP
100g/3½oz/heaped
  ⅓ cup caster sugar
1 tbsp honey
1 tsp lemon juice

This dish, which is called *galaktoboureko* in Greek, is equally as good without the rhubarb if the season isn't right. Instead you could make it with extra filling – and perhaps some orange blossom extract in the syrup.

Preheat the oven to 200°C/400°F/Gas 6 and lightly grease a baking tray with butter. Cut the rhubarb into 20cm/8in lengths and put on the baking tray with any shorter pieces. Sprinkle over the sugar and bake in the oven for 15 minutes. Remove from the oven, leaving the oven on.

Meanwhile, to make the custard filling, put the milk, vanilla extract, semolina, sugar and eggs in a heavy-based saucepan over a medium-low heat. Stirring constantly, heat slowly until thickened, without letting the mixture boil. This will take about 15 minutes. Remove from the heat and leave to one side.

Lay a sheet of filo pastry on the work surface and brush it with some of the melted butter. Put a second sheet on top and brush with more butter, then repeat with 2 more sheets of filo. Line a square 20cm/8in baking dish with the buttered filo, pressing it into the corners, then put the rhubarb on top and pour over the custard. Butter the remaining 6 sheets of filo, stacking them as you go. Put the filo stack over the custard, tucking it in around the edges.

Using a sharp knife, cut the filo and custard into 6 large squares, then cut each square into 2 triangles. Put in the oven and bake for 40 minutes, or until cooked through and the pastry is crisp and golden.

Meanwhile, to make the syrup, put all the ingredients plus 100ml/3½fl oz/ scant ½ cup water in a saucepan and bring to the boil. Reduce the heat to low and simmer, stirring continuously, until the sugar dissolves. Leave to one side.

Remove the dish from the oven, pour over the syrup and leave to cool slightly. Serve warm.

Milk Chocolate & Sea Salt Caramel Pots

PREPARATION TIME: 15 minutes, plus 3 hours setting time | COOKING TIME: 10 minutes | SERVES: 4

SEA SALT CARAMEL
200g/7oz/scant 1 cup
   caster sugar
200ml/7fl oz/generous
   ¾ cup double cream
a large pinch of sea salt
1 egg yolk

MILK CHOCOLATE CREAM
300ml/10½fl oz/scant
   1¼ cups double cream
1 tsp vanilla extract
300g/10½oz milk
   chocolate, very flnely
   chopped
2 egg yolks

CARAMEL SHARDS
300g/10½oz/scant
   1⅓ cups caster sugar
1 tbsp sea salt crystals

To make the sea salt caramel, stir the sugar and about 1 tablespoon water in a saucepan over a high heat until dissolved, then bring to the boil. Reduce the heat to low and simmer until the sugar starts to caramelize and turn golden. Watch the pan closely because the sugar turns very dark very quickly. Also, try not to get any sugar crystals on the side of the pan, as they will cause the caramel to crystallize.

Remove from the heat, add the cream and salt and mix until well combined. The cream will bubble and the caramelized sugar may start to go hard – if it does, return the pan to a low heat and stir constantly until it dissolves and the ingredients are incorporated. Remove from the heat and leave to cool slightly, then whisk in the egg yolk. Pour the caramel into four 150ml/5fl oz/scant ⅔ cup glass serving bowls or ramekins and put in the fridge for 1 hour to set.

To make the milk chocolate cream, put the cream and vanilla extract in a saucepan over a medium-high heat and bring just to the boil, then remove from the heat and add the chocolate. Stir until completely melted, then leave to one side for 5 minutes to cool slightly before whisking in the egg yolks. Remove the ramekins from the fridge and pour the chocolate cream over the top. Return to the fridge to set for 1–2 hours.

To make the caramel shards, first line a baking tray with baking parchment. Using the sugar and 50ml/1¾fl oz/scant ¼ cup water, follow the method above for caramelizing the sugar. Pour immediately onto the prepared baking tray, sprinkle the sea salt crystals over the top and leave to one side to harden.

To serve, break the sheet of caramel into shards and use to decorate each caramel pot.

Pomegranate Panna Cottas with Redcurrant & Orange Salad

PREPARATION TIME: 20 minutes, plus 3 hours setting time or overnight | COOKING TIME: 3 minutes | SERVES: 4

6 gelatine sheets
150ml/5fl oz/scant ⅔ cup double cream
150ml/5fl oz/scant ⅔ cup milk
300ml/10½fl oz/scant 1¼ cups pomegranate juice
3 tbsp grenadine
50g/1¾oz/scant ¼ cup fruit sugar or caster sugar

REDCURRANT & ORANGE SALAD
2 oranges
200g/7oz redcurrants

It's probably obvious by now that pomegranate is one of my favourite ingredients! These pink wobbly panna cottas are a little different from the usual dessert.

Soak the gelatine sheets in a small bowl of cold water for about 5 minutes until softened. Meanwhile, put the cream, milk, pomegranate juice, grenadine and fruit sugar in a saucepan over a medium-high heat and bring to just below boiling point, then remove from the heat. Squeeze the gelatine sheets to remove any excess water and stir into the pomegranate mixture until dissolved.

Pour into four individual metal pudding moulds, about 200ml/7fl oz/generous ¾ cup capacity, if you want to turn the panna cottas out onto dessert plates, or into four pretty serving bowls, if not. Put in the fridge to set for at least 3 hours, or overnight.

One hour before serving, make the redcurrant and orange salad. Using a sharp knife, peel the oranges, removing all the skin and pith, then cut in half and carefully cut into segments.

If the panna cottas are in metal moulds, pour boiling water into a bowl and quickly dip the moulds into the water before turning them upside down on to dessert plates. Arrange the redcurrants and orange on top and around the panna cottas. If the panna cottas are in serving bowls, pile the fruit salad into the middle of the bowls and serve.

"Beautiful and delicious, these fruity panna cottas make a great end to a meal."

Caramelized Coconut Rice Pudding

PREPARATION TIME: **15 minutes** | COOKING TIME: **1 hour 10 minutes** | SERVES: **4**

25g/1oz butter
50g/1¾oz/¼ cup light
  soft brown sugar
100g/3½oz/scant ½ cup
  pudding rice
400ml/14fl oz/generous
  1½ cups coconut milk
250ml/9fl oz/1 cup milk
4 tsp Malibu rum
1 small coconut

TO SERVE
lime wedges

This dessert was inspired by my time in Asia. The caramelized, almost palm sugar-like flavour mixed with the rich coconut rice is soothing and comforting. It makes a great finale to a spicy feast.

Preheat the oven to 160°C/325°F/Gas 3. Melt the butter in a large, ovenproof saucepan over a medium-low heat, then add the sugar and cook for 5–8 minutes until caramelized and bubbling. Stir in the rice, coconut milk, milk and Malibu. The mixture may clump up and stick together at this point, but don't worry.

Cover the pan with a tight-fitting lid, or line the lid with foil and set it on top, and bake in the oven for 30 minutes. Remove from the oven and stir well, then return to the oven for a further 30 minutes, or until the rice is cooked through and the sauce is thick and creamy.

Towards the end of the cooking time, preheat the grill to high. Pierce the circles at the top of the coconut and drain out the liquid, then crack the coconut in half using a meat mallet, rolling pin or hammer. Using a swivel-bladed vegetable peeler, slice out shavings of coconut and lay on a baking tray. Slide the tray under the grill and toast the shavings for a few minutes until golden brown.

Remove the rice pudding from the oven and serve with the toasted coconut shavings sprinkled over the top and lime wedges on the side for squeezing over. Store any coconut shavings not used in an airtight container in a cool place for up to 3 weeks. They are also great for decorating the Coconut & Lime Cake on page 189.

Cassia-Scented Custard Tart with Apple Compote

PREPARATION TIME: 20 minutes, plus making the pastry | COOKING TIME: 1 hour 30 minutes | SERVES: 8

1 recipe quantity Sweet
  Shortcrust Pastry (see
  page 202)
1 vanilla pod
750ml/26fl oz/3 cups
  double cream
2 x 5cm/2in pieces of
  cassia bark
150g/5½oz/heaped
  ⅔ cup caster sugar
4 eggs, plus 4 egg yolks,
  reserving a little egg
  white for brushing
1 tsp ground cinnamon

APPLE COMPOTE
4 crisp green apples,
  such as Granny Smith,
  peeled, cored and
  thickly sliced
100g/3½oz/generous
  ¾ cup sultanas
1 tsp lemon juice
50g/1¾oz/¼ cup caster
  sugar

Preheat the oven to 180°C/350°F/Gas 4. Roll out the pastry on a lightly floured surface until about 3mm/⅛in thick and large enough to line a 25cm/10in tart tin with a 2cm/¾in overlap. Carefully lift the pastry into the tart tin, then press the pastry into the flutes so the pastry comes above the tin. Line the inside of the pastry with baking parchment, weighted down with pastry weights or rice.

Put in the oven and bake for 20 minutes, then remove the parchment and weights, prick the base with a fork and brush with beaten egg white and return to the oven for a further 5 minutes until just starting to turn golden. Remove the pastry case from the oven and reduce the temperature to 140°C/275°F/Gas 1.

Meanwhile, using a sharp knife, split the vanilla pod in half and scrape the seeds into a saucepan with the cream and cassia bark. Bring slowly to the boil. Reduce the heat and simmer gently for 4 minutes to infuse.

Meanwhile, using an electric beater, whisk the sugar, eggs and egg yolks together in a bowl until light and fluffy. When the cream is ready, slowly pour it into the bowl, whisking continuously until well combined. Pour the mixture through a fine sieve into a jug or bowl, removing the cassia bark and any other lumps, then pour the mixture into the pastry case and spread out in an even layer. Put the tart in the oven and bake for 40–50 minutes until just set and still quite wobbly. Remove from the oven and leave to one side to cool before trimming the pastry to the height of the tin with a sharp knife.

To make the apple compote, put the apples, sultanas, lemon juice and sugar in a saucepan over a medium-high heat. Bring to the boil, then reduce the heat to low and simmer for 10 minutes. Leave to one side to cool. Serve slices of the tart with spoonfuls of the compote.

Pimm's Trifle

PREPARATION TIME: 20 minutes, plus 15 minutes cooling time, 3½ hours setting time | COOKING TIME: 15 minutes |
SERVES: 4-6

8 trifle biscuits or
　16 savoiardi or
　lady finger biscuits
200ml/7fl oz/generous
　¾ cup double cream

ENGLISH CUSTARD
1 vanilla pod
3 egg yolks
150g/5½oz/heaped
　⅔ cup caster sugar
1 tbsp cornflour
300ml/10½fl oz/scant
　1¼ cups full-fat milk
100ml/3½fl oz/scant
　½ cup double cream

PIMM'S JELLY
8 gelatine sheets
200ml/7fl oz/generous
　¾ cup Pimm's No. 1
600ml/21fl oz/scant
　2½ cups lemonade
1 small handful of micro
　mint, plus extra to
　decorate
300g/10½oz
　strawberries

There is nothing more English than Pimm's, apart from maybe the classic trifle. This dessert combines the two and is great for a sun-filled summertime treat.

To make the Pimm's jelly, soak the gelatine sheets in a small bowl of cold water for about 5 minutes until softened. Mix the Pimm's and lemonade together in a large bowl, then pour 100ml/3½fl oz/scant ½ cup of the mixture into a small saucepan. Bring just to the boil, then remove from the heat immediately. Squeeze the gelatine sheets to remove any excess water, then stir into the heated Pimm's mixture until dissolved. Add the gelatine mix to the remaining cold Pimm's mix and then stir in the micro mint and strawberries.

Line a serving bowl with the trifle biscuits, then pour over the strawberry jelly. Leave to cool, then cover with clear film and put in the fridge to set for 3 hours.

To make the English custard, using a sharp knife, split the vanilla pod in half and scrape the seeds into a heatproof bowl. Add the egg yolks, sugar and cornflour and whisk together until combined. Pour the milk and cream into a non-stick saucepan and bring to the boil, then pour into the egg yolk mixture, stirring continuously so the eggs don't cook. Pour the custard mixture back into the saucepan and heat very gently, stirring continuously, until thickened. Leave the custard to one side until cool.

Pour the cooled custard over the set jelly and return the bowl to the fridge for 30 minutes until the custard has set.

Pour the cream into a bowl and whisk until soft peaks form, then spoon over the custard. Decorate with a sprinkling of micro mint and serve.

Maple Syrup Cheesecake

PREPARATION TIME: 20 minutes and minimum 6 hours setting time | COOKING TIME: 50 minutes | SERVES: 8

100g/3½oz butter,
  softened, plus extra
  for greasing
1kg/2lb 4oz cream
  cheese, softened
2 tbsp cornflour
100g/3½oz/heaped
  ⅓ cup caster sugar
250ml/9fl oz/1 cup maple
  syrup, plus extra for
  drizzling
1 vanilla pod
6 eggs
400ml/14fl oz/generous
  1½ cups double cream
1 tsp lemon juice

TO DECORATE
2 persimmons, quartered,
6 physalis, some in their
  casings
50g/1¾oz/¼ cup pecan
  nuts

This is quick to cook and pretty foolproof. Unlike most cheesecakes, it doesn't have a base: it's just a large slab of creamy richness. The maple syrup adds caramel overtones and the pecans add crunch.

Preheat the oven to 180°C/350°F/Gas 4. Lightly grease a 25cm/10in springform cake tin, then wrap the base tightly with foil and put the tin in a roasting dish.

Using an electric beater, mix together the butter, cream cheese, cornflour, sugar and maple syrup until well combined. Using a sharp knife, split the vanilla pod in half and scrape the seeds into the butter mixture. Stir until the seeds are evenly mixed through.

Add the eggs one at a time to the cream cheese mixture, beating well after each addition, then pour in the cream and lemon juice and beat until all the ingredients are well combined.

Pour the cream cheese mixture into the prepared cake tin and then pour boiling water into the roasting dish until it comes two-thirds of the way up the sides of the cake tin. Put in the oven and bake for 35 minutes, then turn the heat up to 200°C/400°F/Gas 6 and cook for a further 15 minutes, or until just set and golden around the edges.

Remove from the oven and leave to cool to room temperature, then cover with clear film and put in the fridge to set for at least 6 hours, or overnight.

Remove the cheesecake from the tin and set on a serving plate. Decorate the top of the cheesecake with the persimmons, physalis and pecans and lightly drizzle over some maple syrup.

"A no-fuss cheesecake that tastes divine."

Mont Blanc Semifreddo

PREPARATION TIME: 20 minutes, plus 2 hours freezing time or overnight | COOKING TIME: 2 hours 15 minutes | SERVES: 8

4 eggs, separated
450g/1lb/scant 2 cups
   caster sugar
1 tsp cornflour
500ml/17fl oz/2 cups
   double cream
1 vanilla pod
25ml/1fl oz brandy
300g/10½oz sweetened
   chestnut purée

TO SERVE
150g/5½oz dark
   chocolate (optional)

Preheat the oven to 140°C/275°F/Gas 1. Line two baking sheets with baking parchment then, using the base of a 25cm/10in springform cake tin as a guide, trace out two large circles. Line the springform tin with baking parchment.

Put the egg whites in a large, clean bowl and whisk, using an electric beater, until soft peaks form. Gradually add 250g/9oz/heaped 1 cup of the sugar, a spoonful at a time, whisking continuously, until all the sugar has been incorporated and is dissolved and the mixture is thick and glossy. Beat in the cornflour.

Pipe or spoon the meringue onto the baking sheets inside the traced circles, leaving a gap of about 1cm/½in to allow for the meringue to expand. Put the meringue discs in the oven and bake for 2 hours until crisp, then remove from the oven and transfer to a wire cooling rack to cool completely.

Put the cream in a large, clean bowl and whisk, using an electric beater, until soft peaks form. Using a small sharp knife, split the vanilla pod in half and scrape the seeds into the bowl. Mix until well combined. Leave to one side.

Put the egg yolks, brandy and remaining sugar in a heatproof bowl and rest the bowl over a saucepan of gently boiling water, making sure the bottom of the bowl doesn't touch the water. Using a hand-held electric beater, whisk for 10–15 minutes until the mixture is thick enough to leave a trail. Fold the egg yolk mixture into the whipped cream and then fold in the chestnut purée. Don't mix the purée in completely, as it looks nicer if you leave a few trails of it.

Put one meringue disc in the springform tin, then spoon in the chestnut cream mixture. Top with the second meringue disc, then cover with foil and freeze for at least 2 hours or overnight. Remove from the freezer 10 minutes before serving.

Put the chocolate (if using) in a heatproof bowl and rest it over a saucepan of gently simmering water, making sure the bottom of the bowl doesn't touch the water. Heat, stirring occasionally, until the chocolate has melted. Drizzle over the dessert before serving.

Mango with Micro Basil Sorbet

PREPARATION TIME: 10 minutes, plus 30 minutes churning time and minimum 2 hours freezing time | COOKING TIME: 10 minutes | SERVES: 4

250g/9oz/heaped 1 cup
    caster sugar
50g/1¾oz micro basil
    leaves, plus 1 large
    handful
1 tbsp lime juice
2 mangoes

This simple dish is very good as a dessert after a rich Asian dish. Micro basil has more of an aniseed flavour than normal basil, and it makes a palate-cleansing finale. You can, of course, use normal basil or Thai basil if you prefer.

Put the sugar and 50g/1¾oz micro basil into a saucepan with 250ml/9fl oz/ 1 cup water and bring to the boil. Turn the heat down and simmer for 10 minutes to infuse the liquid with the basil. Remove from the heat, add the lime juice and then strain through a fine sieve into a jug or bowl. Leave to one side to cool. When the syrup Is cold, add the remaining basil.

To make the sorbet using an ice-cream machine, pour the syrup into the bowl and churn according to the manufacturer's instructions until it forms a sorbet consistency. This will take about 30 minutes. Spoon the sorbet into a plastic or metal container and put in the freezer for at least 2 hours.

Alternatively, to make the sorbet by hand, pour the syrup into a plastic or metal container that has been chilled in the freezer. Cover and freeze for 1½ hours, then remove from the freezer and stir the frozen edges into the rest of the mixture. Refreeze and then repeat the process at hourly intervals 2 or 3 more times until completely frozen and of a sorbet consistency. (Note that the sorbet will not be quite as smooth as if made using an ice-cream machine.)

Using a sharp knife, carefully slice each mango down both sides, avoiding the stone. Peel the skin off the mango sides, then cut the flesh into slices. Peel the remaining parts of the mango and slice the flesh from the stone. Serve the mango topped with large scoops of the sorbet.

Ginger Jellies with Plum Purée & Micro Coriander

PREPARATION TIME: 15 minutes, plus 5 hours setting time | COOKING TIME: 15 minutes | SERVES: 4

9 gelatine sheets
800ml/28fl oz/3¼ cups
 ginger ale
10 purple plums, stones
 removed and cut into
 quarters
100g/3½oz/heaped
 ⅓ cup caster sugar
1 small handful of micro
 coriander

I get asked to make a lot of healthy food for clients, and these desserts are perfect because they are fat free and can be made with fruit sugar to reduce the GI levels too. Coriander may sound a bit odd here, but it does work, believe me.

Soak the gelatine sheets in a bowl of cold water for about 5 minutes until softened. Pour 150ml/5fl oz/scant ⅔ cup of the ginger ale into a saucepan and bring to the boil. Remove the pan from the heat immediately. Squeeze the gelatine sheets to remove any excess water, stir into the ginger ale until dissolved and then pour the mixture into four 125ml/4fl oz/¼ cup pudding bowls. Put in the fridge for 4–5 hours until set.

Meanwhile, put the plums, sugar and 100ml/3½fl oz/scant ½ cup water in a saucepan over a medium-high heat and bring to the boil. Reduce the heat to low and simmer for about 10 minutes until the plums are softened. Tip into a blender or food processor and blitz to a purée, then pass through a fine sieve into a bowl. Cover with clear film and put in the fridge to chill until the jellies are ready.

Turn the jellies out onto four plates. Spoon the plum purée lightly over the jellies, then sprinkle over the micro coriander to serve.

Poached Peaches with Honey Cream

PREPARATION TIME: 5 minutes | COOKING TIME: 25 minutes | SERVES: 4

4 white peaches
200g/7oz/scant 1 cup
   caster sugar
200ml/7fl oz/generous
   ¾ cup double cream
1 tbsp clear honey

TO SERVE
pistachio biscotti
   (optional)

This dish relies on the beauty of the produce, so make it when fragrant white peaches are in season. You can also serve it with Greek yogurt for a healthy breakfast dish. The peaches can be served warm or cold.

Pour 500ml/17fl oz/2 cups water into a saucepan, add the sugar and bring to the boil. Add the peaches, then reduce the heat to low and simmer for 10 minutes until the peaches are softened. Remove the peaches from the pan and then simmer the liquid for 15 minutes until thick and syrupy. Pour the syrup over the peaches and leave to one side.

Pour the cream into a bowl and whisk until soft peaks form. Add the honey and briefly whisk again to combine. Serve the peaches with the honey cream and the syrup drizzled over, and with pistachio biscotti, if you like.

Blood Orange Tart

PREPARATION TIME: 20 minutes, plus making the pastry | COOKING TIME: 1 hour | SERVES: 8

1 recipe quantity Sweet
   Shortcrust Pastry
   (see page 202)
plain flour, for dusting
200g/7oz/scant 1 cup
   caster sugar
7 eggs, plus 3 egg yolks,
   reserving a little egg
   white for brushing
juice and zest of 2 lemons
200ml/7fl oz/generous
   ¾ cup blood orange juice
200ml/7fl oz/generous
   ¾ cup double cream

TO SERVE
crème fraîche

The classic lemon tart is one of life's best inventions, but I wanted to make something slightly different. Blood oranges are beautiful but have quite a short season, though you can get the juice all year round. The result is a slightly softer citrus tart with a hint of blush.

Preheat the oven to 180°C/350°F/Gas 4. Roll out the pastry on a lightly floured surface until about 3mm/⅛in thick and large enough to line a 25cm/10in deep tart tin with 2cm/¾in overlay. Carefully lift the pastry into the tart tin, then press the pastry into the flutes so the pastry comes above the tin. Line the inside of the pastry with baking parchment, weighted down with pastry weights or rice.

Put in the oven and bake for 20 minutes, then remove the paper and weights, prick the base with a fork and brush with beaten egg white and return to the oven for a further 5 minutes until just starting to turn golden. Remove the pastry case from the oven and reduce the temperature to 140°C/275°F/Gas 1.

In a large bowl, and using an electric beater, whisk the sugar, eggs and egg yolks together, then add the lemon juice and zest, orange juice and cream and whisk until well combined.

Pour the citrus mixture through a fine sieve into a jug or bowl, removing the zest and any lumps, then pour the mixture into the pastry case and spread out in an even layer. Put the tart into the oven for 30 minutes, or until just set and still quite wobbly. Leave to cool before trimming the pastry to the height of the tin with a sharp knife. Serve with a dollop of crème fraîche.

Nectarine & Vanilla Clafoutis

PREPARATION TIME: 15 minutes | COOKING TIME: 30 minutes | SERVES: 4

butter, for greasing
2 nectarines, pitted
   and diced
3 eggs
60g/2¼oz/scant ⅓ cup
   caster sugar, plus extra
   for sprinkling
300ml/10½fl oz/scant
   1¼ cups milk
60g/2¼oz/½ cup
   self-raising flour
a pinch of sea salt
2 tsp vanilla extract
1 vanilla pod

Clafoutis is a classic French dessert that is surprisingly easy to make. It is usually made with cherries, but I love using ripe nectarines. It is the ultimate seasonal dessert, as it works with blackberries, raspberries and gooseberries too.

Preheat the oven to 180°C/350°F/Gas 4. Grease a 1l/35fl oz/4 cup ovenproof glass or ceramic baking dish with butter and arrange the nectarine pieces over the base. Using an electric beater, beat together the eggs and sugar in a bowl until light and fluffy, then add the milk and vanilla extract and beat until well incorporated. Using a sharp knife, split the vanilla pod in half and scrape the seeds into the egg and sugar mixture. Beat again until the seeds are evenly mixed through.

Sift the flour and salt into the batter, then very gently fold the flour through until well combined. Pour the batter over the nectarines. Put the dish in the oven and cook for 30 minutes until golden and risen.

Remove from the oven, sprinkle over caster sugar and serve immediately. It will deflate a little, which is fine and to be expected.

Raspberry & Pistachio Meringue Pie

PREPARATION TIME: 20 minutes, plus making the pastry | COOKING TIME: 45 minutes | SERVES: 8

1 recipe quantity
   Sweet Shortcrust Pastry
   (see page 202)
plain flour, for dusting
500g/1lb 2oz raspberries
7 egg whites
300g/10½oz/scant
   1⅓ cups caster sugar
1 tsp cornflour
2 tsp nibbed or chopped
   pistachio nuts

This is a quick version of the beloved lemon meringue pie. The raspberries piled up in a pre-baked pastry case provide the tartness against the sweet meringue and pistachios.

Preheat the oven to 180°C/350°F/Gas 4. Roll out the pastry on a lightly floured surface until about 3mm/⅛in thick and large enough to line a 20cm/8in deep loose-bottom tart tin with a 2cm/¾in overlay. Carefully lift the pastry into the tart tin, then press the pastry into the flutes so the pastry comes above the tin. Line the inside of the pastry with baking parchment, weighted down with pastry weights or rice.

Put in the oven and bake for 20 minutes, then remove the paper and weights and prick the base with a fork. Whisk one of the egg whites with a fork and brush it over the pastry base. Return the tin to the oven for a further 5 minutes until just starting to turn golden. Remove from the oven and allow to cool a little, before trimming the pastry to the height of the tin with a sharp knife. Line the base with the raspberries.

Meanwhile, put the remaining egg whites in a large clean bowl and whisk, using an electric beater, until soft peaks form. Gradually add the sugar, a spoonful at a time, whisking continuously until all the sugar has been incorporated and is dissolved and the mixture is thick and glossy. Finally, whisk in the cornflour.

Spoon the meringue mixture over the raspberries, piling it in the middle to form a high peak, then sprinkle over the pistachios. Bake in the oven for 20 minutes until the meringue top is lightly golden. Remove from the oven and leave to cool before serving at room temperature.

Rose Water Pavlova

PREPARATION TIME: **25 minutes** | COOKING TIME: **2 hours** | SERVES: **4**

6 large egg whites
150g/5½oz/heaped
  ⅔ cup caster sugar
1 tsp cornflour
1 tsp rose water, plus an
  extra splash
a drizzle of Grenadine
  syrup
300ml/10½fl oz/scant
  1¼ cups double cream
1 tsp vanilla extract
200g/7oz raspberries

TO SERVE
1 small handful of rose
  petals (optional)

I adore dream-like, feminine desserts – dishes that wouldn't look out of place in a fairytale or wonderland setting. This pavlova, with its pillows of rose-scented cream, raspberries and crisp pink meringue, is a show stopper and it tastes magical, too.

Preheat the oven to 140°C/275°F/Gas 1 and line two baking trays with baking parchment. Put the egg whites in a large mixing bowl, then, using an electric beater, whisk until soft peaks form. Adding a spoonful at a time, whisk the sugar into the egg white until the meringue is thick and glossy. Add the cornflour, rose water and Grenadine and mix well.

Spoon the meringue mixture into a pastry bag and pipe a 20–25cm/8–10in disc on each of two lined baking trays. Use the remaining mixture to pipe small meringues around the meringue discs. Put the trays in the oven and bake for 1½ hours. Remove the mini meringues from the oven and leave to one side to cool. Continue to bake the meringue discs for a further 30 minutes, then remove from the oven and leave to cool.

When the meringues are cold, whip the cream together with a splash of rose water and the vanilla extract until soft peaks form.

Put one of the meringue discs on a serving plate and cover with half the cream and raspberries. Place the second disc on top and cover with the remaining cream, then decorate with the remaining raspberries and the mini meringues. To finish, sprinkle over the rose petals. (These are edible, but if you prefer not to eat them, just remove.)

Goat's Cheese, Quince & Micro Celery Stacks

PREPARATION TIME: 15 minutes | COOKING TIME: 15 minutes | SERVES: 4

1 long thin French
  baguette
1 tsp olive oil
400g/14oz rindless
  goat's cheese
1 tbsp crème fraîche
200g/7oz quince paste
100g/3½oz micro celery
  shoots
freshly ground black
  pepper

Sometimes I don't feel like making a sweet dessert but neither do I want a straight-up cheese board and biscuits. This is just right for those days: little layers of creamy goat's cheese, slivers of quince and micro celery shoots for a savoury delight.

Preheat the oven to 200°C/400°F/Gas 6. Cut the baguette on the diagonal into 12 very thin and long slices and lay the pieces on a baking tray. Drizzle over the oil. Put in the oven and bake for 10–15 minutes until golden brown. Remove from the oven and leave to one side to cool.

Meanwhile, put the goat's cheese and crème fraîche in a bowl and beat until it forms a piping consistency. Season with pepper. Cut the quince paste into slices of a similar size to the slices of baguette.

Spoon the goat's cheese mixture into a pastry bag and pipe about 1 heaped teaspoon onto a slice of toasted baguette. Put a slice of quince paste on the goat's cheese, then another slice of toast, some more cheese and another slice of quince paste. Repeat once more, then finish with a little more cheese and sprinkle on one-quarter of the celery shoots. Make up the remaining 3 stacks and serve.

Sfakian Cheese Pies

PREPARATION TIME: 45 minutes, plus 1 hour rising time | COOKING TIME: 40 minutes | MAKES: 8

1 egg
55ml/1¾fl oz/scant
  ¼ cup olive oil
500g/1lb 2oz/4 cups
  plain flour, plus extra
  for dusting
1 tsp salt
500g/1lb 2oz mizithra or
  ricotta cheese
oil, for frying

TO SERVE
strong Greek clear honey,
thyme leaves
edible flowers (optional)

These pies are renowned in Crete, where they are mainly made in a remote area on the south of the island. While they do take some time to master, the thin bread with cheese in the middle, drizzled with honey, really takes some beating. I couldn't resist including them.

Whisk together the egg, oil and 125ml/4fl oz/½ cup water in a jug. Sift the flour and salt into a large bowl. Make a well in the flour, then pour in the liquid mixture and knead the dry and wet ingredients together with your hands to make a smooth dough. Cover with a damp tea towel and leave to rest in a warm, draught-free place for 1 hour.

Divide the dough into 8 pieces and roll each piece into a ball on a lightly floured surface and flatten slightly. Divide the mizithra or ricotta cheese into 8 pieces and put one portion in the centre of each dough ball. Wrap the dough around the cheese until it is completely covered.

Preheat the oven to 150°C/300°F/Gas 2 and put a baking sheet in to warm. Take one dough ball, press down to flatten and then very gently and carefully roll it into a thin pancake until about the size of a side plate. Turn the dough as you roll and make sure the cheese doesn't come out. Repeat with the remaining dough balls.

To cook the pies, heat a little oil in two frying pans over a medium heat, then fry one pie in each pan for about 5 minutes on each side until lightly browned. Keep them warm in the oven while you cook the remaining 6 pies.

Serve drizzled with honey and sprinkled with thyme leaves and edible flowers, if you like.

Wild Mushroom- & Truffle-Filled Camembert

PREPARATION TIME: 20 minutes, plus 1 hour chilling time and 30 minutes resting time | SERVES: 4

30g/1oz dried wild
  mushrooms
100g/3½oz cream cheese
2 tsp truffle oil
250g/9oz Camembert
  cheese
sea salt and freshly
  ground black pepper

TO SERVE
crackers or French bread
  stick

I used to make a version of this in one of the Michelin-starred restaurants I worked in as a teenager. It's a wonderful combo of wild mushroom, truffle and cheese, and it oozes flavour.

Put the mushrooms in a heatproof bowl and pour over boiling water to cover. Leave to soak for 10 minutes, then drain, chop the mushrooms finely and put back in the bowl.

Add the cream cheese and truffle oil to the mushrooms and season with salt and pepper. Mix until thoroughly combined.

Cut the Camembert in half horizontally, then sandwich the cream cheese mixture between the two halves. Cover with clear film and put in the fridge to chill for 1 hour.

Remove the stuffed Camembert from the fridge at least 30 minutes before serving to bring it to room temperature. Serve with crackers or slices of crusty French bread.

"If you bought this in a deli, it would cost a fortune!"

Baking

Za'atar Flatbreads

PREPARATION TIME: 40 minutes, plus 2½ hours proving time | COOKING TIME: 1 hour 5 minutes | MAKES: 8

1 tsp dried active yeast
360g/12¾oz/heaped
  2⅓ cups wholemeal
  flour
150g/5½oz/scant
  1¼ cups strong white
  flour, plus extra for
  dusting
1 tsp fine sea salt
2 tbsp cornflour

ZA'ATAR MIX
2 tbsp toasted sesame
  seeds
2 tsp dried thyme
2 tsp chopped fresh
  thyme
2 tsp sumac
1 tsp sea salt crystals

Dissolve the yeast with 250ml/9fl oz/1 cup lukewarm water in a small jug. Sift the wholemeal and strong white flours together into a large bowl (tipping in the bran left in the sieve) and add the salt.

Make a well in the centre of the flours, then pour in the yeast mixture and knead the dry and wet ingredients together with your hands to make a soft dough – you may need to add another 1–2 tablespoons water if it is too dry. Turn the dough onto a lightly floured surface and knead for a further 5–10 minutes, or until smooth and elastic. Put the dough in a bowl lightly dusted with flour, cover with a damp, clean tea towel and leave to prove in a warm, draught-free place for 1½–2 hours, or until the dough has doubled in size.

Meanwhile, mix all the ingredients for the za'atar mix together in a bowl.

Knock the air out of the dough, turn it out onto a lightly floured surface and mould into a long sausage shape. Pinch off 8 equal-sized pieces of dough, roll each dough piece into a ball and then roll the dough balls in the cornflour until coated all over. Put the balls on a baking tray lightly dusted with flour, cover with a damp, clean tea towel and put in the warm, draught-free place for a further 30 minutes.

On a clean surface, press down a dough ball with the palm of your hand a few times, rotating the dough a little after each press. Pick up the flattened piece of dough and shift it from one hand to the other, using a swift motion, to stretch it. Put the dough back on the surface and, using a rolling pin, roll it out as thinly as possible. Repeat for the remaining dough balls.

Heat a large nonstick frying pan over a medium heat, then put a flatbread in the pan and cook for 5 minutes until browned. Flip over the bread, spread over a teaspoon of the za'atar mix and cook for a further 3 minutes, or until cooked through. Repeat for the remaining flatbreads, piling them up under a damp tea towel as they are cooked to keep warm before serving.

Chilli & Coriander Cornbread

PREPARATION TIME: 15 minutes | COOKING TIME: 20 minutes | SERVES: 4

125g/4½oz butter, melted, plus extra for greasing
125g/4½oz/heaped ½ cup caster sugar
2 eggs
280ml/9½fl oz/scant 1¼ cups buttermilk
½ tsp bicarbonate of soda
250g/9oz/2 cups self-raising flour
250g/9oz/1⅔ cups fine cornmeal
½ tsp salt
1 tbsp chopped pickled jalapeño chilli
1 small handful of micro coriander
125g/4½oz grated Cheddar cheese

Cornbread was one of the first breads I learnt to make as a child, and its buttery goodness has been a firm favourite ever since. There are lots of different styles, and this is a simple and very quick one that should be eaten while warm. Try adding additional flavours, such as bacon pieces, chillies, various cheeses, etc.

Preheat the oven to 180°C/350°F/Gas 4 and grease a 33 x 20cm/13 x 8in baking tin with plenty of butter. Beat the butter and sugar together in a large bowl, then add the eggs, one at a time, mixing well after each addition.

Pour the buttermilk into a separate bowl, add the bicarbonate of soda and stir well, then stir into the sugar mixture. Sift in the flour, add the cornmeal and salt and stir until well combined. Finally add the chilli, micro coriander and Cheddar.

Pour the cornbread mix into the prepared tin, put in the oven and bake for 20 minutes or until risen and golden brown. Remove the cornbread from the oven and cool slightly in the tin, then cut into wedges and serve warm.

Oaty Soda Bread

PREPARATION TIME: 15 minutes | COOKING TIME: 30 minutes | MAKES: 1 loaf

250g/9oz/1²/₃ cups
   wholemeal flour
200g/7oz/scant 1²/₃ cups
   plain flour, plus extra
   for dusting
50g/1¾oz/heaped ¹/₃ cup
   oatmeal
1 tsp bicarbonate of soda
1 tsp caster sugar
1 tsp salt
50g/1¾oz butter, melted
400ml/14fl oz/generous
   1½ cups buttermilk
   (or mix together ²/₃ milk
   with ¹/₃ natural yogurt)

Soda bread is another quick bread to make. There really is nothing much better than warm soda bread with butter and jam for breakfast. I have added oats for some extra texture and fibre, which will also keep you fuller for longer.

Preheat the oven to 180°C/350°F/Gas 4. Put the wholemeal and plain flours, oatmeal, bicarbonate of soda, sugar and salt in a large bowl and mix until well combined.

Mix together the butter and buttermilk in a jug. Make a well in the dry ingredients and gradually pour in the buttermilk mix, then bring the dry and wet ingredients together, using your hands, until just combined. Don't overwork the mixture.

Turn the oaty dough out onto a lightly floured surface and mould into a round shape. Cut a deep cross in the centre, dust the top with flour and put on a baking tray. Bake in the oven for 30 minutes until golden brown. Remove from the oven and leave to cool a little on a wire rack. Serve warm.

Cinnamon, Date & Cardamom Buns

PREPARATION TIME: 30 minutes, plus 2½ hours proving time | COOKING TIME: 25 minutes | MAKES: 8

300ml/10½fl oz/scant
   1¼ cups milk
1 tbsp dried active yeast
4 eggs
100g/3½oz/heaped
   ⅓ cup caster sugar
100g/3½oz unsalted
   butter, melted
800g/1lb 12oz/scant
   6⅓ cups plain flour, plus
   extra for dusting

FILLING
2 tbsp cinnamon
1 tsp ground cardamom
200g/7oz dates, chopped
100g/3½oz/scant ½ cup
   demerara sugar
1 tsp vanilla extract
200g/7oz butter

SYRUP
2 tsp cinnamon
200g/7oz/scant 2 cups
   caster sugar

The smell of cinnamon buns seems to have a hypnotic effect on people. Instead of the usual sultanas, I have used toffee-like dates and added a little cardamom, then finished it off with a sticky syrup.

Warm the milk in a saucepan over a medium heat, then stir in the yeast and leave to dissolve.

Put the eggs, caster sugar and butter in a jug and mix together, then whisk in the warmed milk. Sift the flour into a large bowl, make a well in the centre and pour in the yeast mixture, then knead the dry and wet ingredients together to make a rough, sticky dough. Turn the dough out onto a lightly floured work surface and knead for 5 minutes, or until the dough is smooth and elastic.

Put the dough in a clean bowl, cover with a damp tea towel and leave to prove in a warm, draught-free place for 1½–2 hours, or until the dough has doubled in size. Meanwhile, mix together all the dry filling ingredients in a bowl. Put the butter in a saucepan and melt, then tip it into the bowl and stir until well combined. Leave to one side.

Knock the air out of the dough, turn it out onto a lightly floured surface and knead slightly. Roll out until about 1 cm/½in thick, then spread over the filling in an even layer and roll up the dough. Cut into 5cm/2in pieces and arrange the pieces, cut-side up, in a 25cm/10in round cake tin. Cover with a damp tea towel and leave to prove for 30 minutes.

Preheat the oven to 200°C/400°F/Gas 6. Put the buns in the oven and bake for 20 minutes until golden brown and risen. Meanwhile, put the cinnamon, sugar and 100ml/3½fl oz/scant ½ cup water in a saucepan and bring to the boil. Reduce the heat to low and simmer for 10 minutes until slightly thickened. When the buns are cooked, remove from the oven and drizzle over the syrup, leaving them in the cake tin to cool before serving.

Orange Blossom Éclairs

PREPARATION TIME: 25 minutes, plus chilling time | COOKING TIME: 35 minutes | MAKES: 14

oil, for greasing
75g/2½oz/heaped ½ cup
  plain flour, plus extra
  for dusting
50g/1¾oz butter
2 eggs, beaten
200ml/7fl oz/generous
  ¾ cup double cream
50g/1¾oz/scant ½ cup
  icing sugar
1½ tsp orange blossom
  water

ICING
200g/7oz/heaped 1½
  cups fondant icing sugar
  or icing sugar

TO DECORATE
edible gold leaf (optional)

These were inspired by a Middle Eastern dessert called *atayef bi ashta*, which is often served during Ramadan, after the sun has gone down. I adore the orange blossom-flavoured custard and have added some gold leaf for a luxurious Arabic touch.

Preheat the oven to 200°C/400°F/Gas 6 and lightly oil and flour a baking sheet. Pour 150ml/5fl oz/scant ⅔ cup water into a saucepan, add the butter and bring to the boil.

Reduce the heat to medium, then, stirring vigorously and continuously, add the flour in one quick burst. Continue stirring until a soft paste forms and the oil from the butter starts to come to the surface. Remove the saucepan from the heat, then gradually beat in the eggs until the mixture is smooth and glossy and has a dropping consistency. Leave to cool.

Spoon the choux pastry paste into a large piping bag fitted with a 2cm/¾in plain nozzle and pipe 8cm/3¼in lengths on the prepared baking sheet, leaving a space between each for the éclairs to double in size during baking. Put in the oven and bake for 30 minutes until cooked through, golden brown and crispy.

Remove the éclairs from the oven, pierce the bottoms with a skewer to release the steam and leave on a wire cooling rack until cold.

Whip the cream and icing sugar together in a bowl, until stiff peaks form. Mix in the orange blossom water, then spoon the cream into a piping bag fitted with a plain nozzle. Pierce the base of each éclair with the piping nozzle and pipe the cream into the éclairs. Put in the fridge to chill.

To make the icing, mix together the icing sugar and 1 tablespoon water in a bowl. Dip the top of the éclairs in the icing or spread the icing using a palette knife. Leave to set, then sprinkle with edible gold leaf, if you like, before serving.

Iced Fancies

PREPARATION TIME: 1 hour | COOKING TIME: 50 minutes | MAKES: 16

50g/1¾oz butter, melted and cooled, plus extra for greasing
4 eggs
100g/3½oz/heaped ⅓ cup caster sugar
½ tsp almond extract
50g/1¾oz/heaped ⅓ cup cornflour
50g/1¾oz/heaped ⅓ cup self-raising flour
75g/2½oz raspberry jam, warmed
150g/5½oz marzipan
icing sugar, for dusting

FONDANT ICING
500g/1lb 2oz/4 cups fondant icing sugar
pink, green, blue and yellow food colouring

Preheat the oven to 180°C/350°F/Gas 4 and grease and line a 20cm/8in square cake tin with baking parchment. Break the eggs into a large heatproof bowl, add the sugar and rest the bowl over a saucepan of simmering water, making sure the bottom of the bowl doesn't touch the water. Using a hand-held electric beater, whisk for 5–8 minutes until the mixture doubles in size.

Remove the bowl from the heat, add the butter and almond extract and stir until well combined. Then, using a metal spoon, very gently fold in the flours. Pour the mixture into the prepared cake tin.

Put the cake in the oven and bake for 30–40 minutes until lightly golden and a skewer inserted into the centre comes out clean. Remove the cake from the oven and turn it out onto a wire cooling rack to cool completely. When cold, slice in half horizontally and sandwich the 2 halves together with the jam, reserving 1 tablespoon. Trim off the edges and cut into sixteen 5 x 5cm/ 2 x 2in squares.

Roll the marzipan out on a surface lightly dusted with icing sugar until about 3mm/⅛in thick, then spread the reserved jam evenly over the top. Cut the marzipan into 16 squares to fit the tops of the individual cakes and put one piece, jam-side down, on each cake.

To make the fondant icing, mix the fondant icing sugar with enough hot water to make a smooth icing of a thick pouring consistency. Divide the icing into four separate bowls and mix a few drops of food colouring into each bowl to make up soft pastel pink, green, blue and yellow icings. Cover the bowls with clear film to prevent the icing forming a skin.

Put the cakes on a wire cooling rack over a baking tray, then, one by one, uncover each bowl and pour a coloured icing over one-quarter of the cakes, using a palette knife to smooth it down the sides. Leave to set before serving.

"These gorgeous pastel-coloured, bite-sized cakes are just perfect for afternoon tea."

Coconut & Lime Cake

PREPARATION TIME: 25 minutes, plus making the coconut shavings | COOKING TIME: 35 minutes | SERVES: 8

225g/8oz unsalted butter,
softened, plus extra
for greasing
225g/8oz/scant 1 cup
caster sugar
4 eggs
zest of 1 lime
150g/5½oz block of
creamed coconut,
grated
3 tbsp coconut milk
225g/8oz/scant 1¾ cups
self-raising flour

ICING
200g/7oz/heaped ¾ cup
caster sugar
2 egg whites
1 tbsp Malibu rum

TO DECORATE
25g/1oz toasted coconut
shavings (see page 154)

Coconut and lime go so well together. The creamed coconut makes a very moist sponge and the icing is light and fluffy.

Preheat the oven to 180°C/350°F/Gas 4 and grease and line a 23cm/9in round cake tin with baking parchment. Using an electric mixer, beat together the butter and sugar in a bowl until light and fluffy.

Whisk the eggs together in a separate bowl, then gradually add to the creamed butter mixture, a little at a time, beating well after each addition to prevent the mixture curdling. Beat in the lime zest (reserving a few strands for decorating) and creamed coconut, followed by the milk, then gently fold in the flour until everything is well combined.

Pour the mixture into the prepared cake tin, put in the oven and bake for 30 minutes, or until golden and a skewer inserted into the centre comes out clean. Remove from the oven and turn out onto a wire cooling rack to cool completely before icing.

To make the icing, put the sugar in a saucepan with 4 tbsp water and stir to dissolve, then bring to the boil and then boil for 4 minutes to form a syrup. Meanwhile, whisk the egg whites in a large, clean bowl until firm. Pouring in a slow, steady stream, add the sugar syrup to the egg whites, whisking continuously until the meringue is thick and glossy. Finally, whisk in the Malibu.

Slice the cake in half horizontally and place the bottom half on a serving plate. Sandwich the two halves together with a thick layer of the warm icing, then cover the sides and top with the remaining icing. Decorate with the coconut shavings and the reserved lime zest. Leave to cool before serving.

Rich Flourless Chocolate Cake

PREPARATION TIME: 20 minutes, plus 45 minutes cooling | COOKING TIME: 35 minutes | SERVES: 8

225g/8oz unsalted butter, softened, plus extra for greasing
200g/7oz dark chocolate, 50% cocoa solids
4 eggs, separated
200g/7oz/scant 1 cup caster sugar or 1 cup fruit sugar
1 tsp sea salt crystals
1 tsp vanilla extract

TO SERVE
200ml/7fl oz/generous ¾ cup crème fraîche

I try to avoid eating much wheat and I have had many clients who do the same, so here is no-flour cake. I have also suggested using fruit sugar here as it is a healthier option. This cake is super rich and decadent. Serve with a dollop of crème fraîche.

Preheat the oven to 160°C/325°F/Gas 3 and grease and line a 15cm/6in round cake tin with baking parchment. Put the chocolate and butter in a heatproof bowl and rest it over a saucepan of gently simmering water, making sure the bottom of the bowl doesn't touch the water. Heat, stirring occasionally, until the chocolate and butter have melted. Put to one side.

Using an electric mixer, beat together the egg yolks and half of the sugar until the mixture is pale and thick.

Put the egg whites in a separate clean, large bowl and whisk until soft peaks form, then gradually add the remaining sugar, a spoonful at a time, and the salt, whisking continuously until all the sugar has been incorporated and is dissolved and the mixture is thick and glossy.

Stir the melted chocolate and butter into the egg yolk mixture, then add the vanilla extract and gently fold in the egg whites until well combined.

Pour the mixture into the prepared cake tin, put in the oven and bake for 30 minutes, or until firm to the touch and a skewer inserted into the centre of the cake comes out clean. Remove the cake from the oven and turn out onto a wire rack to cool completely.

Serve with crème fraîche either at room temperature or after chilling the cake in the fridge for a more dense texture.

Lemon Meringue Cupcakes

PREPARATION TIME: 25 minutes | COOKING TIME: 20 minutes | MAKES: 10

110g/3¾oz butter, softened
110g/3¾oz caster sugar
2 eggs
1 tsp vanilla extract
100g/3½oz self-raising flour
½ tsp baking powder
2 tbsp milk
100g/3½oz/generous ⅓ cup lemon curd

MERINGUE
2 egg whites
115g/4oz/heaped ½ cup caster sugar

Cupcakes are still very popular and I have seen some mad creations. Here, the combination of soft sponge with lemon curd and meringue topping is simply lovely.

Preheat the oven to 180°C/350°F/Gas 4 and line a 12-cup muffin tray with paper liners. Using an electric mixer, beat together the butter and sugar until light and fluffy.

Whisk the eggs together in a separate bowl, then gradually add to the creamed butter mixture, a little at a time, beating well between each addition to prevent the mixture curdling. Beat in the vanilla extract.

Sift the flour and baking powder together into the wet ingredients and gently fold in until all the flour has been incorporated. Finally, fold in the milk. Spoon the mixture into the muffin cases, filling each one about two-thirds full. Put in the oven and bake for 10 minutes, or until risen and golden brown.

Remove the cupcakes from the oven, leaving the oven on. Allow the cupcakes to cool slightly, then scoop out (and discard) a teaspoon of cake from the middle of each cake and spoon 1–2 heaped teaspoons lemon curd into each hole.

To make the meringue, put the egg whites in a dry, clean bowl and whisk until soft peaks form, then gradually add the sugar, a spoonful at a time, whisking continuously, until all the sugar has been incorporated and is dissolved and the mixture is thick and glossy.

Spoon the meringue into a piping bag fitted with a plain nozzle, then neatly pipe a little mound of the meringue over the lemon curd on the cupcakes, leaving a gap around the edges. Put the cupcakes back into the oven for 10 minutes, or until the meringue tops are lightly golden. Remove from the oven and leave to cool.

Mayan Chocolate Cupcakes

PREPARATION TIME: 25 minutes | COOKING TIME: 20 minutes | MAKES: 12

110g/3¾oz unsalted
   butter, softened
110g/3¾oz/heaped
   ½ cup light brown
   muscovado sugar
100g/3½oz dark
   chocolate, 70% cocoa
   solids
2 eggs
1 tsp vanilla extract
1 red chilli, deseeded and
   finely diced
100g/3½oz/heaped
   ¾ cup self-raising flour
½ tsp baking powder
1 tsp cinnamon
1 tsp mixed spice
1 tsp orange zest
2 tbsp milk

ICING
300ml/10½fl oz/scant
   1¼ cups double cream
200g/7oz dark chocolate,
   70% cocoa solids, finely
   chopped
1 tbsp clear honey

TO DECORATE
12 slivers of deseeded
   chilli
12 pink peppercorns
ground cinnamon,
   for sprinkling
edible gold dust, for
   sprinkling (optional)

To make the icing, pour the cream into a saucepan over a medium heat, bring to a gentle boil, then immediately remove the pan from the heat. Stir the chocolate into the cream, mixing until melted, then stir in the honey. Leave to one side to cool for 45 minutes–1 hour until it is a thick, piping consistency.

While the icing is cooling, make the cakes. Preheat the oven to 180°C/350°F/Gas 4 and line a 12-cup muffin tray with paper liners. Using an electric mixer, beat together the butter and sugar until light and fluffy.

Meanwhile, put the chocolate in a heatproof bowl and rest it over a saucepan of gently simmering water, making sure the bottom of the bowl doesn't touch the water. Heat, stirring occasionally, until the chocolate has melted. Alternatively, melt the chocolate in a glass bowl in the microwave in 1-minute spurts, checking frequently.

Whisk the eggs together in a separate bowl, then gradually add to the creamed mixture, a little at a time, beating well after each addition to prevent the mixture curdling. Beat in the vanilla extract, melted chocolate and chilli.

Sift the flour, baking powder, cinnamon and mixed spice together into the wet ingredients, add the orange zest and gently fold the mixture until all the dry ingredients have been incorporated. Finally, fold in the milk.

Spoon the mixture into the muffin cases, filling each one about two-thirds full. Put in the oven and bake for 10 minutes, or until risen and springy to the touch. Remove from the oven and transfer the cupcakes to a wire cooling rack to cool completely.

Pipe the cooled icing in swirls over the tops of the cupcakes, using a piping bag fitted with a star nozzle. Alternatively, spread the icing over the tops using a palette knife. Decorate each cupcake with 1 sliver of chilli and 1 peppercorn and sprinkle over the cinnamon and edible gold dust, if using before serving.

"The Mayans worshipped chocolate, and magically combined it with chilli and spices."

Caramel Cookie Sandwiches

PREPARATION TIME: 25 minutes, plus 30 minutes chilling time | COOKING TIME: 20 minutes | MAKES: 20

225g/8oz unsalted butter, softened
115g/4oz/scant ²/₃ cup light soft brown sugar
2 egg yolks
300g/10½oz/heaped 2⅓ cups plain flour, sifted, plus extra for dusting
150g/5½oz dulce de leche
fine sea salt (optional)
400g/14oz milk chocolate, chopped

Buttery sable biscuits, sweet caramel and a layer of chocolate... what can I say? The perfect cookies.

Preheat the oven to 160°C/325°F/Gas 3 and line two baking sheets with baking parchment. Using an electric mixer, beat together the butter and sugar until light and fluffy, then add the egg yolks, one at a time, mixing well after each addition.

Add the flour to the butter mixture and mix until it just forms a paste. Do not overmix or the dough will be tough when cooked. Shape the dough into a ball, wrap in clear film and put in the fridge for 30 minutes to firm up.

Roll the chilled dough out on a lightly floured surface until about 5mm/¼in thick. (The dough is very short, so it might be easier to roll it out in batches.) Using a 5.5cm/2½in round cookie cutter, cut out 40 circles and put on the lined baking sheets. Put in the oven and bake for 10–15 minutes until lightly golden. Remove the cookies from the oven and transfer to a wire cooling rack to cool.

When the cookies are cold, sandwich together with a spoonful of the dulce de leche, leaving them on the wire cooking rack. If you like, before sandwiching the cookies together, sprinkle a little sea salt over the dulce de leche.

Put the chocolate in a heatproof bowl and rest it over a saucepan of gently simmering water, making sure the bottom of the bowl doesn't touch the water. Heat, stirring occasionally, until the chocolate has melted. Alternatively, melt the chocolate in a glass bowl in the microwave in 1-minute spurts, checking its progress frequently.

Carefully pour the melted chocolate over the tops of all the cookies. Leave to cool, then transfer to another rack or plate and put in the fridge to set.

Honey Madeleines with Earl Grey Cream

PREPARATION TIME: 20 minutes, plus overnight chilling time | COOKING TIME: 10 minutes | MAKES: 24

4 eggs
100g/3½oz/heaped ¾ cup icing sugar
2 tbsp clear honey
1 tsp orange zest
1 tsp vanilla extract
200g/7oz/scant 1½ cups plain flour, sifted
½ tsp baking powder
250g/9oz unsalted butter, plus extra for greasing, melted

EARL GREY CREAM
2 tsp loose Earl Grey tea leaves
200ml/7fl oz/generous ¾ cup double cream
25g/1oz/scant ¼ cup icing sugar

Madeleines were made famous by Proust and his memories invoked by them. You can tell why – they scent the house with buttery goodness and are best eaten warm. In Greece I serve them with candied bergamot in syrup too.

Put the eggs and sugar in a bowl and whisk, using an electric beater, until light and fluffy and the volume has doubled in size.

Add the honey, orange zest and vanilla extract, then fold in the flour and baking powder until well combined. Stir in the melted butter, then transfer the mixture to a clean container, cover with clear film and leave overnight in the fridge.

Preheat the oven to 180°C/350°F/Gas 4 and brush a 24-cup madeleine tin (or two 12-cup tins) with butter. Spoon the mixture into the moulds until about three-quarters full, then put in the oven and bake for 10 minutes until golden. Remove from the oven and turn the madeleines onto a wire cooling rack to cool a little.

To make the Earl Grey cream, infuse the tea leaves in 3 tablespoons boiling water until the water has cooled. Using an electric beater, whisk the cream and icing sugar together in a bowl until they form stiff peaks. Strain the tea infusion into the cream mixture and beat until combined. Serve with the madeleines.

Basics

The following recipes are used as part of some of the main recipes or as accompaniments. They are also a selection of deliciously handy recipes that will work as part of any number of different meals you may make at home, from your own special pizza and pasta dishes to simply grilled meats and vegetables.

BBQ Sauce

PREPARATION TIME: 5 minutes | COOKING TIME: 50 minutes | MAKES: 500ml/9fl oz/2 cups

1 tsp vegetable oil
2 banana shallots, finely chopped
500ml/17fl oz/2 cups tomato ketchup
150ml/5fl oz/scant 2/3 cup cider vinegar
2 tbsp black molasses
200g/7oz/heaped 1 cup brown sugar
1 tsp cayenne pepper
2 tsp celery salt
2 tsp made English mustard

Heat the oil in a saucepan over a medium heat, then add the shallots and cook gently, covered, so the juices sweat out, for 8 minutes or until softened and translucent. Add the rest of the ingredients and mix well.

Bring to the boil, then reduce the heat to low and simmer very gently, stirring occasionally, for 30–40 minutes until thick and glossy. Because of the high sugar content the mixture will burn easily, so don't be tempted to increase the heat.

The sauce can be kept in an airtight jar for 2–3 weeks.

Dipping Sauce

PREPARATION TIME: 5 minutes

1 red chilli, finely chopped
2.5cm/1in piece of root ginger, peeled and finely chopped
1 tbsp soy sauce
1 tsp fish sauce
1 tsp mirin
2 tbsp rice vinegar

Put all the ingredients in a small bowl and whisk until thoroughly combined.

The sauce can be kept in an airtight jar for 2–3 days.

Mayonnaise

PREPARATION TIME: 10 minutes | MAKES: 300ml/10½fl oz/scant 1¼ cups

2 egg yolks
1 tbsp white wine vinegar
1 tsp Dijon mustard
225ml/7½fl oz/scant
   1 cup vegetable oil
5 tsp olive oil
a squeeze of lemon juice,
   to taste
a pinch of cayenne
   pepper
sea salt
2 garlic cloves, finely
   chopped (optional)

Put the egg yolks, vinegar and mustard in a food processor or blender and blitz until pale. With the motor running, pour in the oil – first the vegetable oil and then the olive oil – very slowly. If you add the oil too quickly, the mayonnaise may split.

When all the oil has been incorporated, add the lemon juice and cayenne pepper, then season with salt.

If making garlic mayonnaise, add the garlic cloves with the mustard.

The mayonnaise can be kept in an airtight jar in the fridge for up to 4 days.

Yogurt Sauce

PREPARATION TIME: 5 minutes | MAKES: 300ml/10½fl oz/scant 1¼ cups

200g/7oz/scant 1 cup
   Greek yogurt
1 garlic clove, finely
   chopped
1 tsp clear honey
1 tbsp tahini

Put all the ingredients into a jug or bowl and whisk together until thoroughly combined.

The sauce is best used on the day it is made.

Pineapple & Chilli Sambal

PREPARATION TIME: 10 minutes | SERVES: 4

1 shallot, finely sliced
1 red chilli, deseeded and
   finely sliced
300g/10½oz pineapple,
   peeled, "eyes" removed,
   cored and cut into small
   pieces

Put all the ingredients in a large bowl and toss until well combined.

The sambal is best used on the day it is made.

Curry Paste

PREPARATION TIME: 5 minutes

5cm/2in piece of root
 ginger, roughly chopped
2 large shallots
4 garlic cloves
1 red chilli, deseeded
2.5cm/1in piece of
 galangal, peeled and
 sliced
½ tsp turmeric
½ tsp ground cumin
½ tsp ground coriander
½ tsp chilli powder
2 tbsp coconut milk

Put all the ingredients in a blender or food processor and blitz until very smooth.

The paste is best used on the day it is made but can be kept in an airtight jar for 2–3 days.

Quick Tomato Chutney

PREPARATION TIME: 5 minutes | COOKING TIME: 40 minutes | MAKES: 600g/1lb 5oz/generous 2 cups

2 banana shallots,
 chopped
800g/1lb 12oz tinned
 chopped tomatoes
1 tsp yellow mustard
 seeds
½ tsp smoked paprika
200g/7oz/heaped 1 cup
 brown sugar
150ml/5fl oz/scant ⅔ cup
 white wine vinegar
½ tsp sea salt

Put all the ingredients in a large saucepan and bring to the boil. Reduce the heat to low and simmer, stirring occasionally, for 40 minutes or until reduced, thick and glossy. Remove from the heat and leave to one side to cool.

The chutney can be kept in an airtight jar for 2–3 weeks.

Deluxe Burger Buns

PREPARATION TIME: 30 minutes, plus 4 hours proving time | COOKING TIME: 40 minutes | MAKES: 8 buns

3 tbsp milk, warmed
1 tsp sugar
2 tsp dried active yeast
450g/1lb/scant 3²/₃ cups
    bread flour, plus extra
    for dusting
1 tsp salt
2 tbsp butter
1 egg and 1 egg yolk
sesame seeds, poppy
    seeds or black onion
    seeds, for sprinkling

Mix together the milk, 250ml/9fl oz/1 cup warm water, the sugar and yeast in a small bowl and leave to sit for 5 minutes. Sift the flour and salt into a large bowl, then rub in the butter with your fingertips until the mixture resembles fine breadcrumbs.

Whisk the egg into the yeast mixture. Make a well in the flour mixture, then pour in the yeast mixture and knead the dry and wet ingredients together, using your hands, to make a rough, sticky dough. Turn the dough out onto a lightly floured work surface and knead for a further 10 minutes, or until the dough is smooth and elastic.

Put the dough in a clean, oiled bowl, and lightly oil the dough. Cover with a damp tea towel and leave in a warm, draught-free place for 1¹/₂–2 hours, or until the dough has doubled in size.

Line a baking sheet with parchment paper or oil and lightly dust with flour. Knock the air out of the dough, turn out onto a lightly floured work surface and knead again for 5 minutes. Divide the dough into 8 pieces, knead a little more and then mould into bun shapes. Put the dough pieces at least 5cm/2in apart on the baking sheet, cover with a tea towel and leave to one side for a further 1¹/₂–2 hours. The buns need to be a lot bigger before they are cooked, so don't be tempted to rush this proving stage otherwise they will be tough.

Preheat the oven to 180°C/350°F/Gas 4 and put a baking dish filled with water on the bottom; this is to create moisture and keep the crust chewy. Brush the buns with the egg yolk and sprinkle with sesame seeds, poppy seeds or black onion seeds, as preferred. Bake for 30–40 minutes until golden brown, then transfer to a wire rack to cool.

Note that for my Lobster Rolls with Pea Shoots (see page 66), you need to form the dough into hot-dog rolls rather than round buns.

Flatbreads

PREPARATION TIME: 15 minutes, plus 15 minutes resting time | COOKING TIME: 15 minutes | MAKES: 4

400g/14oz/3¼ cups strong bread flour, ideally 00 plain flour, plus extra for dusting
1 egg, beaten
250g/9oz/1 cup natural yogurt
generous 3 tbsp olive oil, plus extra for oiling
sea salt

Put all the ingredients in a stand mixer with a dough hook and mix to a smooth dough. Turn the dough into a lightly oiled bowl, cover with clear film and put in the fridge for at least 15 minutes. If you want, you can make the dough the day before and leave in the fridge overnight.

Roll and bake the flatbreads according to the recipes on pages 43 and 179. Alternatively, if making plain flatbreads, preheat the oven to 180°C/350°F/ Gas 4. Roll the dough out on a lightly floured surface, then divide the dough according to the size of flatbread required and flatten into discs. Put the discs on a baking tray and bake for 10–15 minutes or until golden brown.

Sweet Shortcrust Pastry Dough

PREPARATION TIME: 10 minutes, plus 30 minutes chilling time | MAKES: 375g/13oz

120g/4¼oz butter, softened
50g/1¾oz/scant ¼ cup caster sugar
1 vanilla pod
1 large egg
200g/7oz/heaped 1½ cups plain flour, plus extra for dusting

Put the butter and sugar in a mixing bowl. Using a sharp knife, split the vanilla pod in half and scrape the seeds into the bowl. Using an electric beater, beat the ingredients together until smooth.

Add the egg and beat briefly until incorporated into the butter mixture, then add the flour and beat until just combined. Don't overbeat mixture or the pastry will toughen.

Turn the pastry dough out onto a lightly dusted work surface and quickly shape it into a ball. Cover in clear film and chill for at least 30 minutes before using.

Pasta Dough

PREPARATION TIME: 40 minutes, plus 30 minutes resting time | SERVES: 4

600g/1lb 5oz/5 cups 00 plain flour, plus extra for dusting
1 tsp sea salt
5 eggs, plus 1 egg yolk for brushing
1 tbsp olive oil

Sift the flour and salt into a pile on a clean work surface, then make a well in the centre of the flour. Whisk the eggs and olive oil together in a small bowl or jug, then pour the liquid into the well. Using your hands, gradually bring the flour into the centre to start to form a rough dough, then knead the dough until it is smooth. Shape into a ball, wrap in clear film and put in the fridge to rest for 30 minutes.

Now you need to gradually roll the dough until it is about 3mm/⅛in thick. If you have a pasta machine, it is quite fun, but if you are going to use a rolling pin, it does take some dedication.

If using a pasta machine, cut the dough in half and set one half to one side under a damp tea towel. Roll out the first half on a lightly floured surface until about 1cm/½in thick. Set the pasta machine up according to the manufacturer's instructions, ensuring it is securely attached to a clean work surface with lots of space around it. Set the machine to its widest setting, dust the rollers and the work surface with flour and then start to feed the pasta into the machine. Roll the dough through the machine once, then fold it in half and roll It again. Fold the dough in half, turn the machine down a setting and then roll the dough twice on this setting, folding it in half each time. At this point you will probably have to cut the sheet in half because of its size; cover the remaining sheets with a damp tea towel while you carry on rolling so that they don't get too dry. Turn the machine down another setting and roll the dough twice more. Continue until you have rolled the dough through the finest setting twice. Repeat with the remaining half of the dough.

If making ravioli, use the whole sheets of pasta. If making fettucine, tagliatelle or other pasta shapes, either pass the dough through the pasta machine using the correct cutting attachment, or fold the sheets in half a few times and cut with a knife, using a ruler to keep the strips even.

Pizza Dough

PREPARATION TIME: 30 minutes, plus minimum 2 hours proving time | MAKES: 4 small pizzas or 1 large pizza

1 tbsp active dried yeast
500g/1lb 2oz/4 cups
   strong bread flour,
   ideally 00 flour, plus
   extra for dusting
1 tsp caster sugar
1 tbsp sea salt
3 tbsp olive oil
fine semolina, for dusting

Mix the yeast with 375ml/13fl oz/1½ cups warm water in a small bowl. Put the flour, sugar and salt in a large bowl and mix well. Make a well in the centre of the flour mixture, then pour in the yeast mixture and the olive oil, and knead the dry and wet ingredients together, using your hands, to make a rough dough. Turn the dough out onto a lightly floured work surface and knead for a further 10 minutes, or until the dough is smooth and elastic. Put the dough in a clean, oiled bowl, and lightly oil the dough. Cover with a damp, clean tea towel and leave to prove in a warm, draught-free place for about 2 hours, or until the dough has doubled in size.

Knock the air out of the pizza dough and knead for 5 minutes, but this time on a surface lightly dusted with semolina. Divide the dough into four pieces for larger individual pizzas (or eight for smaller pizzas) and roll out into discs until about 5mm/¼in thick, or much thinner if a thin base is preferred. If making one large pizza, keep the dough as one piece and roll to a similar thickness.

Roast Garlic & Olive Oil Mash

PREPARATION TIME: 10 minutes COOKING TIME: 40 minutes | SERVES: 4

1 whole garlic bulb
600g/1lb 5oz King
   Edward potatoes,
   peeled and cut into
   medium pieces
1 tbsp extra virgin
   olive oil
sea salt and freshly
   ground black pepper

Preheat the oven to 180°C/350°F/Gas 4. Wrap the garlic bulb in foil, place on a baking tray and roast for 40 minutes. Remove from the oven and leave to cool.

Put the potatoes in a saucepan, cover with water and bring to the boil, then simmer for 20 minutes or until cooked and tender. Strain off the water, then mash the potatoes until smooth. Slice the top of the garlic bulb off and squeeze the purée into the mash. Add the olive oil and seasoning, and mix well.

Celeriac Mash

PREPARATION TIME: 10 minutes | COOKING TIME: 20 minutes | SERVES: 4

600g/1lb 5oz celeriac,
  peeled and cut into
  small pieces
50g/1¾oz butter
sea salt and freshly
  ground black pepper

Put the celeriac in a saucepan, cover with water and bring to the boil, then simmer for 20 minutes or until cooked and tender. Strain off the water and put the pan back on the heat for a few minutes until the remaining water has evaporated. Add the butter, season to taste and mash to a fine purée. For a really fine purée, use a stick blender.

Goat's Cheese Mash

PREPARATION TIME: 5 minutes | COOKING TIME: 10 minutes, 20 minutes to cool | SERVES: 4

600g/1lb 5oz floury
  potatoes such as King
  Edwards, peeled and
  cut into medium pieces
150g/5½oz rindless
  goat's cheese
50g/1¾oz butter
sea salt and freshly
  ground black pepper

Put the potatoes in a saucepan, cover with water and bring to the boil, then simmer for 20 minutes or until cooked and tender. Strain off the water and put the pan back on the heat for a few minutes until the remaining water has evaporated. Crumble in the goat's cheese, and mash. Season, then stir in the butter.

Cooked Turkey

PREPARATION TIME: 10 minutes | COOKING TIME: 20 minutes | SERVES: 4

3 x 100g/3½oz boneless,
  skinless turkey breast
  steaks
500ml/17fl oz/2 cups
  chicken stock

Put the turkey in a saucepan, cover with the stock and bring to the boil. Reduce the heat to low and simmer, covered, for 10 minutes. Remove the pan from the heat and leave to one side for the turkey to cool in the stock. When cooled, remove the turkey from the stock and tear into bite-sized chunks.

Index

208 LOVE GOOD FOOD